Tales from The River Bank

Tales from The River Bank

John Bailey

BBC BOOKS

To Joy…
Joy in the valleys, in the rivers, in the fish that swim them…
and to Mike Gunton and his team for portraying them so faithfully for us all.

This book is published to accompany the BBC television series *Tales from the River Bank*.
Series producer: Michael Gunton

Published by BBC Books
an imprint of BBC Worldwide Publishing
BBC Worldwide Limited, Woodlands, 80 Wood Lane, London W12 0TT

First published 1997
© John Bailey 1997
The moral right of the author has been asserted.

All photographs by John Bailey except for those on the following pages:
118-119 (Johnny Jensen), 142 and 150-151 (Alan Broderick),
146 (Jim Tyree) and 163 (Matt Hayes)

ISBN: 0 563 38798 X

Designed and illustrated by Robert Olsen and Kevan Kelsey of Vista Design

Printed and bound in Great Britain by Butler and Tanner Limited, Frome and London
Jacket printed by Lawrence Allen Limited,
Weston-super-Mare
Colour separations by Radstock Reproductions Ltd, Midsomer Norton

Tales from The River Bank

LEFT: *A superb summer's day when any angler might be forgiven for sitting back and enjoying the sun. This particular swim has been well chosen; the angler is fishing a deep hole at the tail of a fast run of water. Here the barbel and chub remain invigorated as the flow of oxygen sweeps around them and they can also hide from the bright light if necessary. Another advantage of the swim is that the quick current dislodges items of food under the gravel and sends them down to the waiting fish.*

Acknowledgements Thanks first are due to Michael Gunton, whose idea it was to produce this book, Rupert Barrington, Susan McMillan, Mary Summerill, Tim Martin, Hugh Pearson, Liz Appleby, Clare Flegg, Karen Hewson, Yvonne Cattermole, and everyone else on the *River Bank* team in Bristol for their help, understanding and patience. I would also like to thank Kevin Flag and Steve Packham at the Avonmouth Studios for allowing me to flit in and out and no doubt ruin their work schedules. I owe a great debt to the fishermen that have been of such massive help to me – notably Peter Smith, Chris Yates, Chris Rowe, Chris Bennett, Christopher West, Moc Morgan and Charles Jardine. Their support, ideas and encouragement have been of tremendous help to me. Whilst filming, Tom Cook, Paul Van Vlissingen, Derek Darville and Anne Laurance have been generous in every possible way. Can I also thank Anne Voss Barke and David Pilkington at the Arundel Arms, Margeret Jaffrey and Roddy Tee at the Banchory Lodge and all at Dryburgh Abbey Hotel for their generous help with the salmon, trout and sea trout chapters. John Partridge, Peter Drennan, Gary Barclay and Craig Brew have all been massively supportive with help and advice over the tackle and clothing needed for some demanding piscatorial adventures. I must also thank Paul Gustafson in Oxford and the staff at the Freshwater Fishery Laboratory in Fascally, Scotland for their help with some very intricate biological details. Special mention is due to David Overy, Alan Broderick and especially Richie Johnston for their advice on the Irish piking scene. Thanks also to Anna Ottewill and Jane Coney at BBC Books, and to Robert Olsen for his design and illustrations.

Finally, I thank my wife, Joy, for all her help with proofreading, her advice, her photographic ability and her general love and support through many weeks of travelling, and where would I be without Sylvia Hollingworth for coping so magnificently with such an unruly manuscript? Thank you to all.

Introduction

South-west Greenland. August 1995. Air temperatures between 10°C and 14°C, both day and night.

Believe this or not, but the story that follows is the absolute truth. I was trekking in Greenland, following a river from its mouth at the fjord to its source under the towering icecap. Apart from my fishing companion, Johnny Jensen, I didn't see another person or even any sign of a human being for a full ten days, though we were wandering through ancient hunting grounds that had been used by Eskimos for thousands of years. They, like us, had visited this valley in the short summer of the Midnight Sun to catch the Arctic char, as they ran up the crystal river from the sea to spawn. Of course, we have char in the glacial lakes of Britain, but these fish are infinitely more dramatic. Perhaps it is the majestic backdrop of mountain and icecap, or their marine diet of prawns and herring, or even the glow imparted by the snow-melt water, but there is something spellbinding about these char.

The normal pattern of our days was to walk until almost midnight, pitch camp, catch a char, cook it and then sleep for six or seven hours as the sun sank to the rim of the world. This particular night, it was my turn to catch the fish, while Johnny put up the tent and hunted for firewood. Catching my char this night took longer than I had expected, largely because I found myself revelling at the glow of the low sun on the mountain sides. I did not wish to break the perfect peace of the scene with even the screech of a fly reel. When I did catch a char, it too was perfection: a large female with pearly sides and back and a gentle pink glow to her belly. I hardly noticed at first, but some of her scales were very slightly scuffed, perhaps from a brush with a polar bear's claws, or knocked by rocks as she ascended a waterfall. Once spotted, however, the scuffed scales were quite prominent and they shone golden in the light as I turned the char this way and that. I suddenly realized that the marks resembled three letters: G O D.

LEFT: Arctic Greenland and one of the most awe-inspiring rivers in the world. There is perfect peace here, not a soul for hundreds of miles, and the only creatures to plod the tundra are musk ox, Arctic fox, reindeer and elk. This is one of the greatest advantages of fishing: it can take an angler to some of the most wonderful places on earth.

I know that I had been on a diet of fish for over a week and that I had walked a long way on an empty stomach, but there was no doubting either my eyesight or my mind that night. A ridiculous story you might think: surely the letters should have been written in the native Innuit, or even Danish! Nor is God generally in the habit of signing his works of art. Whatever, we carried on and cooked the fish, reasoning that we were as much God's creations as the char.

That night, in my sleeping bag, my thoughts kept turning to that fish and its strange markings. Perhaps it had something to do with being in such a wonderful and haunted place. Outside the tent, the river gurgled and the Arctic foxes snarled over the remains of our supper – no doubt gorging on the skin and bones of the fish in question.

At about 03.00 in the morning, it began to dawn on me that all my life I had been in touch with magic. Even aged four, when I saw my first

ABOVE: Any fisherman will be amazed at the beauty of this huge, fresh run, male Arctic char. As the fish is about to spawn its body takes on a fabulous sheen of orange and its jaw becomes hooked and mean, capable of hauling lesser contenders for the spawning redds out of his way. There are Arctic char in the United Kingdom too but here they have become landlocked and, although very beautiful, cannot compete with the glory of the sea-running fish.

sea trout in the dampness of a Welsh dawn, I marvelled at how its silver drew the light like a polished sword falling through the air. A year later, I caught my first roach in a shrimping net and kept it in a tank in my bedroom. For two days, I admired my silver and scarlet treasure from every angle and in every light. Then I made the acquaintance of some tiny perch: bristling, pugnacious little fish in a livery of black barring on olive, with spiky dorsal fins. The first pike I ever saw was dead, but awesome and terrifying nonetheless. I counted every fleck on its flank and fingered every wicked tooth, quite mesmerized, unable to tear myself away even though it was getting late on a drizzling winter afternoon.

So, whilst my friends were car watching, train spotting or stamp collecting, I considered myself the lucky one. I immersed myself in the watery world of fish and fishing: drinking in mystery and magic, sensing that the objects of my desires were infinitely noble, constantly intriguing, eternally amazing and always beautiful.

There were painful frustrations though. I just couldn't catch enough fish! Soon I realized that if this were to change, I had really to get to know the fish I sought to catch. I began to read absolutely everything that I could lay my hands on about fish and catching them. I talked to older anglers that I met on the towpaths of the canals and beside the ponds near my home. Above all, I began to study the fish themselves. Every day of the school holidays would find me peering into streams and pools: through bushes and reeds; from up trees and bridges; even wading out into the water, way past the tops of my Wellingtons. Perhaps, I thought, I might absorb some of the spirit of the water by actual immersion in it!

All the anglers that I now respect started in a similar fashion. What is more, they have never really changed. Grey-bearded men with Ph.Ds stare into rivers with the same thrill and passion as they had when they were jam jar toting youngsters in short pants. When Mike Gunton and his team from the BBC Natural History Unit wanted to make a series about British freshwater fish, they came to fishermen as well as biologists for the project. Whilst the scientist knows the dry facts of a fish – how many eggs it lays and at what temperature for example – it is the lifelong angler who knows exactly how the trout or the tench behaves, day in, day out, under sun or moon. A good fisherman is a good naturalist. What catches a fish is not expensive tackle, nor complex rigs and fancy baits, but a thorough understanding of the quarry and its mysterious world beneath the surface of the water.

I am sure that anglers will enjoy these programmes. Moreover, many fishers will learn a great deal from the series that is of practical use. They will gain a better understanding of fish which will help them catch better fish in greater numbers. In compiling this book, I have been greatly privileged to travel so widely and meet many gifted anglers. They have been unstintingly generous in passing on the experiences and knowledge gained over lifetimes of fishing. In addition, I have been enormously impressed by the efforts the BBC has made to film fish underwater. Personally, I have found the results profoundly inspiring. The unique underwater footage will give the angler valuable insights into the habits of fish and will show exactly how his quarry behave in certain circumstances – how they react to suspicious baits, or to the sound of a spinner hitting the water's surface for example. I suspect that many long-held suspicions will be confirmed; many equally long-standing myths will be debunked and, perhaps, a good few angling problems solved. But, even if you are not an angler, I am sure you will enjoy the series and this book. If nothing else, it reveals splendidly the great beauty of our lovely native freshwater fish.

Chapter 1

Barbel & Chub
The River Fisher

THE ANGLER SEEKING TO CATCH BARBEL AND CHUB WITH any regularity needs to have more than a degree of understanding of these species. These fish are not often caught with anything less than a dedicated and careful approach. Other coarse fish – roach, rudd, bream and even tench – can be caught almost by accident, but this rarely happens with barbel and chub. They are simply too wary to be caught out by casual techniques. Indeed, they can often give the impression of being almost uncannily perceptive.

I remember well a friend and I spotting three big chub through binoculars, some hundred metres upstream in a clear river. We wanted a closer look and, making a big detour into the meadow, crawled the last few metres on hands and knees. As we neared the bank, we were actually on our bellies and carefully peeked over the edge to look down into the water. All we saw was a glimpse of three big, black-tinged tails as they disappeared. Whether or not they had actually got wind of our presence is hard to tell, but those three enormous chub chose exactly the right moment to depart and we didn't see them again for the rest of the day. I and my friends have scores of similar tales attesting to the almost extra-sensory perceptiveness of chub and barbel.

It is very early morning and there is barely a glimmer of the coming day in the dark sky. Bats are still around and the smell of fox hangs heavily in the moist woodland. There is no breeze and the river slides past like mercury. I leave the wood, cross a potato field and get down to the water's edge itself. I must wade over here to reach the northern bank and I do so cautiously, prodding my landing net handle out in front of me before each step. It is easy enough to veer off course in the gloom and stumble down into deep, dangerous water. Swans are already grazing on

LEFT: The sight every barbel angler wants to see: a large fish rolling towards the net, beaten at last. Look at the closest pectoral fin positioned just behind the fish's gill-flap and waving beneath the water surface. The green, round blemish on it is a water louse, a parasite of barbel. Water lice lurk in the silt on the riverbed from where they transfer themselves to their hosts, colonizing their fins and underbody.

the drifting ranunculus beds. Small chub and trout squirt away from my boot, arrowing up the shallows.

On the far bank, I have a half-mile walk along the edge of the cornfield to a stretch that holds a vast shoal of barbel: a group of around two hundred fish that I found early in the summer. I have fished for them sparingly. Indeed, this is only my fourth trip after these barbel and I never catch more than a single fish on each occasion. It is a rarity these days to find a large shoal of barbel almost undisturbed by angling pressure and far too precious to spoil through overfishing on my part. Free from the regular assaults of anglers, these particular fish behave in as near as possible a natural and wild manner.

I am too early and sit for a while amongst the loosestrife, waiting for the light to grow. On the far bank, I notice the old dog fox I'd winded earlier as he drops down onto the little gravel beach. Unaware of my presence, he sits on his haunches and scratches his ear so vigorously that I can hear the paw rubbing on the coarse fur.

As the sky lightens, the first buzzard mews and then, the sign that I am awaiting. A few metres from my feet a large red-finned barbel rolls porpoise-like out of the water, so slowly that, for a second, I can stare deep into its eye. The shoal is still in residence and, on the evidence of this rolling fish, earnestly about their feeding. Soon, I am able to see a great stain of clouded water, two hundred metres long, drifting off down the current. It looks almost as if some murky effluent were being discharged into the river, but is in fact the silt disturbed by a couple of hundred large barbel rooting for food in the gravel. I continue to watch and in the growing light more is revealed to me. Here and there in the shallows the tips of fins flicker briefly as fish stand on their heads in an effort to dislodge the stones and 'hoover' up caddis grubs, leeches, snails and small fry. The barbel are rolling more frequently now. This usually is a sign that feeding is either about to begin or, probably in this case, coming to an end. If I am going to fish, I'll need to be quick about it, but I am reluctant to miss witnessing such a fascinating spectacle.

The sun, now above the horizon, is just catching the bellies of fish as they turn on their sides and flash on the bottom. This 'flashing' is a most interesting phenomenon and the subject of much debate amongst barbel anglers. Most agree that feeding fish flash consistently, very possibly to dislodge food from the stones. Since this would seem most likely to be of benefit to other fish, stationed downstream, it may be evidence of a co-operative activity for mutual benefit within the shoal.

Flashing may be associated with activities other than feeding. Large male barbel seem to flash as a territorial signal at breeding time and it may have some other signalling function within the shoal. Another theory is that barbel rub their flanks along the stones of the river bed to dislodge small irritating skin parasites. Noticeably, barbel also seem to flash when excited by a change in water temperature.

The sun's heat is on my back now and there is no doubt that the silt cloud is lessening. Fish are leaving the feeding ground, dropping back to stations in mid-river where they will spend the hours of daylight. In front of me, there are probably now less than fifty fish still feeding on the gravel shallows.

In a situation like this, it is hard to beat simple float fishing: setting the float slightly over depth and trundling a big, juicy lobworm along the bottom. Barbel love worms. They are a completely natural bait to use, since every flood washes vast quantities of worms into the river from surrounding farmland. This then is the method I am going to try. I tackle up quickly, bury my size 6 hook into the biggest and most succulent specimen in my worm box and gently swing the tackle out, well upstream of the feeding fish.

Long before the float dips I actually see the barbel sending out a bow wave as it surges towards my worm. The very tip of its dorsal fin knifes through the surface. Momentarily, my float pauses; then travels quickly across the current, before stabbing under. The fight with a decent-sized barbel is dramatic. Powerful, unstoppable runs are interrupted with boring dives to the river bed. When at last the eight-pound fish is drawn gently on its side into the shallow water by the reeds, it is easy to see why. Barbel have sleek powerful bodies and large fins, designed for a life spent in fast water. The pectoral fins are huge hydrodynamic surfaces that seem to be able to clamp the fish onto the gravel bottom, even in an eight-knot current. Though this fish gave a determined fight, even now it can writhe too strongly to be held. Using my artery forceps, I gently unhitch the hook from the corner of its mouth. I right the fish and hold it for a few seconds to recover and get its bearings. Suddenly, with a flick of that huge tail it powerss off into mid-stream, leaving a trail of silt cloud behind it as it goes.

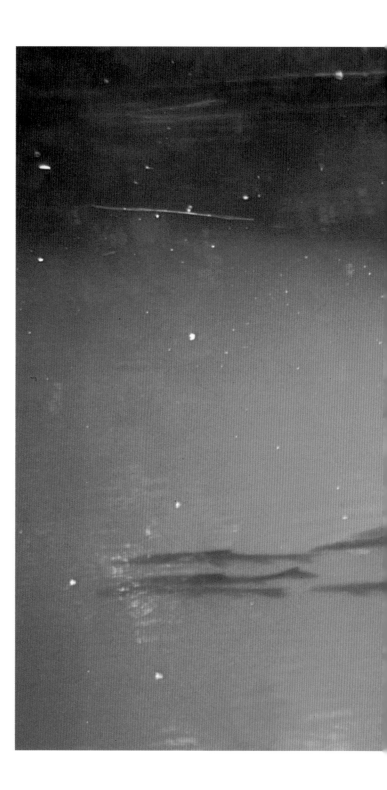

RIGHT: *A very rare sight indeed on any of our barbel rivers: a whole shoal of fish has risen from the bottom to drift in the surface layers, enjoying the warm sunshine. They are rolling and splashing about almost continually, their tails breaking the water's surface. If ever one needed evidence that barbel were a social fish and capable of expressing something like our sense of contentment, here is the proof.*

At mid-morning, I am back at the river. This time I am without fishing tackle, armed instead with polaroid glasses, binoculars and a long lens camera. I find the shoal exactly where I expect it to be: spread out in mid-river, some twenty-five metres from the bank and hanging just under the surface. Fishing lore has it that barbel are bottom-hugging creatures, but they are not always so. Barbel as unpressured by man as these will certainly feed on the bottom, but in the warmer months will often spend a lot of the time in daylight hanging on or near the surface. Just like carp, undisturbed barbel seem to enjoy basking in the sunshine. Whenever the sun is shining, this particular large shoal is nearly always high in the water and easily visible. The only reason that they have escaped discovery and consequent angling pressure is the total remoteness and inaccessibility of this stretch of water. And this is also why these fish behave in a 'natural' way, unlike their brethren in heavily fished waters.

Spending six hours watching such fish is an illuminating experience. One of the first things to notice is the wide variation in colour, which ranges from a pale ivory to almost coal black. In between, barbel can be just about every conceivable shade of orange, bronze and gold. There is no single typical 'barbel colour' and this variety helps considerably in identifying individuals within the shoal and monitoring their particular behaviour patterns.

Watching these fish over a period of time reveals a fascinating pattern of behaviour. The fish tend to keep together and drop downstream at the pace of the current. While doing this, their fins often clear the surface of the water and their bodies roll gently from one side to another, glinting in the sunlight. Occasionally, a large insect – a moth perhaps – is taken from the surface by a fish that rises just like a lazy old brown trout. At other times, a passing shoal of minnows may be harried but, for the greater part of the day, little or no food passes the barbels' lips. A couple of hundred metres downstream, the shoal steadies and stops. Then, it seems as though the same five or six fish swim up from the ranks to the head of the shoal and lead all two hundred barbel back upriver: the group stretched out in a long, thin procession. When the lead fish draw opposite a particular group of alders, they stop. The rest of the shoal then catches up with them and consolidates, whereupon the whole exercise is repeated.

The drift downstream takes around twenty minutes to complete, while the journey back upriver takes about ten minutes. Each tour lasts, therefore, about half-an-hour and is repeated over and over throughout the hours of daylight. During this circuitous behaviour, it appears that particular barbel clan together in smaller companionable groups within the main shoal. These sub-groups are easily recognizable.

Barbel appear to enjoy touching one another: frequently rubbing their bodies together and sometimes curling their dorsal fins over the bodies of their neighbours. I have no doubt, in my own mind, that a barbel shoal operates as a social entity within which there appears a discernible hierarchy. To the best of my knowledge, shoals of 'naturally' behaving barbel like this have hardly ever been witnessed. I have certainly never come across any documented description of such behaviour. Again, I believe that this is almost entirely due to the fact that it is almost impossible in modern-day Britain to find barbel that are undisturbed by angling pressure and other human interference. Most barbel are simply not *allowed* to behave naturally. This is why I only catch one barbel per sortie from this particular shoal and, indeed, rarely even take a rod to these fish.

Moving on to late afternoon and the blistering heat of the day is at last beginning to subside. It is time now to visit a very different, more typical barbel swim. Here, the gradient of the river is steeper. The current is faster and flows swiftly over stones and gravel. Out in mid-stream, there is a great rock that towers above the surface in the low water of summer. I love to sit and fish from this rock, for such large obstructions are very important to barbel. Back eddies and slack spots occur upstream and downstream of such large rocks and offer the barbel some respite from the force of the main current. Fish behaviour tends to be about options and the more possibilities a lie offers a barbel the more it likes it. These eddies also attract minnows and fish fry, as well as acting as traps for other food items and are therefore a magnet for larger fish. Barbel also love sliding their lips along the smooth surface of large rocks, combing the silkweed for the shrimps and snails that live there.

The rock is the ideal position from which to fish. Not only can I control the line perfectly and position the bait with absolute precision, but I can also look into the water and watch exactly what the barbel are doing. Barbel use features like this as temporary resting places when they

LEFT: If possible, a barbel should be lifted as little as possible. Once landed, it should be unhooked and returned to the water in the shallow margins as quickly as possible. Barbel are hardy fish but they give their all in the fight and it is often a good idea to hold them upright against the current for a few minutes to let them regain their strength. Never let a barbel move out into the current unless you are absolutely sure that it has the power to maintain its balance against the stream. If the barbel turns over on its back and rolls away downstream with its belly showing then it is in great danger.

For me, the advantages of touch legering for barbel are manifold and these days I hardly ever use a conventional quivertip.

One advantage of touch legering is that it encourages mobility. You can dispense with rod-rests that have to be driven into the bank, which probably scares the fish. A rod-rest firmly embedded in the bank tends to anchor the angler in one place, both physically and mentally. It is inimical to a roving and adaptable approach.

Another major bonus is that you do not have to stare at a quivertip for hours, possibly missing bites if your attention wanders. Provided you are doing it properly, your fingertips are in constant touch with the hook-bait, via the line. Any touch should register instantly with the angler's brain.

Touch legering gives you the freedom to fish while watching the river for any action. You cannot do this with your eyes glued to a quivertip and sight board! The sight of a rolling barbel a hundred metres downstream will prompt the observant roving angler to go and investigate and – quite probably – find some feeding fish.

Touch legering is really efficient after dark and confers further advantages over other methods. Using your fingertips, you can dispense with a host of bite detection gadgetry, which is usually prone to malfunction anyway. If you are any good at touch legering, your fingertips and brain will be permanently 'switched on'.

Perhaps the greatest advantage of touch legering is that the angler gains a great intimacy with the water through which his end tackle is drifting. You can actually feel the sensation of the bait trundling along the bottom, or being mouthed by a fish. You get none of this intimate contact when using a quivertip. For this reason, touch legering is perfect for pioneering a strange river where you would otherwise be fishing blind.

Nowadays, I hardly ever miss a bite when touch legering. With experience you seem to know instinctively exactly the right moment to hit the fish. With a quivertip, however, I find hooking fish a lot less certain.

There is no hard and fast rule as to how you hold the line to stay in 'touch'. Find a method that suits you. Personally, I hold the rod in my right hand. The line is held in my left hand, running over my index finger and round and underneath my third finger. Keep the line nice and tight to the spool, especially in windy weather. There is nothing worse than hitting into a fish then finding a rogue hitch of line wrapped around the back of the reel.

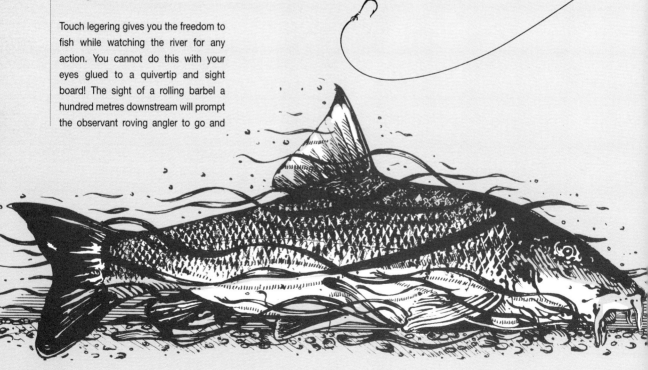

The ideal rod for touch legering is 11 or 12 foot long, with a light but powerful action and a test curve of 1¼ lb to 1½ lb. It should have as few rings as possible (eight or nine rings on a

– 8lb test, depending on the size of the lead and the nature of the water to be fished. Pale grey and olive coloured lines seem to work in clear water and matt nylons may well be less visible than the shiny kinds in bright sunlight. For fish as large and powerful as barbel, hooks have to be strong, especially in the smaller sizes. Specimen hooks such as the Drennan 'Super Specialist', or the

concentration and this cannot be achieved if you are constantly distracted by uncomfortable personal apparel. Standing or sitting, you really need to be able to maintain a fixed position for periods of half-an-hour or more. I never use a seat box these days: I find them too cumbersome. I can usually manage to tuck myself comfortably into some grassy nook.

12-foot rod). A relatively short handle in traditional cork will be found the most handy and comfortable on a rod that has to be held for hours on end. Several tackle companies offer suitable 'specimen' rods in their ranges. If you can't find anything you like 'off the peg', there are several independent specialist rod builders who will make a rod to your exact specifications, often for a surprisingly reasonable sum.

An ordinary fixed-spool reel is ideal for touch legering. It doesn't need wildly sophisticated features, but should be of good quality and have a smooth adjustable drag. The reel line should be good-quality nylon monofilament of 6lb

Kamasan B-980 are hard to better. Sizes range from a 12 for sweet corn, to as large as a 4 for luncheon meat.

Dress the part of the hunter, for camouflage and comfort. Touch legering involves intense protracted

ABOVE: A fascinating underwater shot of barbel tails rippling like fans in the current. This is typical behaviour – barbel love to push together, enjoying the touch of their bodies meeting. It is not unusual to see a whole group of barbel clumped together, especially behind a rock or in some weed where they feel both secure and comfortable.

travel from one stretch of the river to another. Barbel tend to split into two types: the stay-at-homes and the nomads. Very often, the wanderers can be the biggest fish. Virtually every time I fish from here I see several different barbel around me and they are often large. They appear to spend a few hours feeding and resting here before travelling on and, as night falls, the darkness seems to give them a feeling of greater security.

Sometimes, I will fish a natural bait in this situation: a couple of leeches or caddis larvae, or perhaps a dead minnow rolled slowly over the

BELOW: The barbel is a superb fish, ideally suited for life in fast rivers. The slim, torpedo-shape of the fish is perfect for battling quick currents and the large pectoral and ventral fins are invaluable for clamping the fish to gravel beds as the fast water pushes overhead. Its hard, pointed nose is ideal for rooting in the gravel and turning over stones in the hunt for caddis grubs, snails and leeches and its four fleshy barbules, hanging like whiskers around the mouth, are perfect for sensing bullheads, crayfish or any other prey that are trying to lie undetected.

gravel. On other occasions, I like to 'build' the swim: trickle feeding small baits like sweet corn for an hour or more. The aim here is to accustom the fish gradually to a food that they are not usually familiar with. As the barbels' taste for the corn grows, their confidence builds and they start actively hunting for the yellow grains. It is fascinating to watch their growing excitement: to see them rooting round under stones, dislodging the sweet corn with their shoulders and pectoral fins for other fish following behind. As the barbel really become 'hooked' on the sweet corn, fish will roll and even jump as they start intercepting the grains higher up in the water and even on the surface. They become quite manic, wheeling right and left to mop up the grains of corn with almost frenzied gusto.

This evening, I'm using sweet corn: two grains on a small hook (size 12–10). Just a single shot is sufficient to keep the bait dribbling along the bottom in the flow, but not so heavy that it gets stuck in one place. Tonight, there is a big barbel some ten metres below me. Were I to cast too close to him, the splash would make him bolt, probably half-

a-mile downriver. If, on the other hand, I drop the bait in well upstream and let it trundle down towards him, then it shouldn't cause any alarm. He will see it a few metres off, watch it carefully and then, begin to home-in, *if* there is nothing about the bait that spooks him. I can see other, smaller barbel in the clear sunlit water and I lift the bait clear whenever they come close. I'm not here for six-pounders!

The shadows lengthen and at last the sun sinks below the horizon. Visibility becomes increasingly restricted. My concentration is entirely focused on the few square metres of water before me. I will the big ivory fish to make a mistake and suck in the little grains of corn on my hook. I notice several of the smaller fish deserting the swim. They might have been disturbed by my presence on the rock, but I think it more likely that they have become aware of the line in the water, possibly rubbing on the flank of a fish as it passes. Soon, there is just me on the rock, three lesser barbel and a monster beneath. Eventually, darkness descends completely and I am fishing blind. In the woods around, owls hoot continuously and downstream there is a crash in the water. It might be a large salmon, or possibly a pike beginning to hunt the dace along the margins.

As usual, I hold the line between my fingertips, feeling for trembles and the quivering vibration of a barbel's sensitive whiskers gently investigating the bait. Tonight, there is none of that. The line suddenly jabs along my index finger, the rod hoops round and I find myself playing a fish almost before I know it. A great surging pull almost topples me from my perch on the rock and, for a moment, I am sure that I have hooked the big fish. However, I manage to stop it within ten metres: something I could never do with a barbel of twelve pounds or more. Relaxing, I begin to enjoy the fight. Bats flit around me in the dark and one or two actually flick the taut line with their wings as they pass. Eventually, the fish is subdued. As I had guessed, it's not the big one, but a beautiful barbel nonetheless. I play the torchlight briefly up and down its bronzed flanks before slipping it back into the cooling river. I pack up and walk home through grass already heavy with dew.

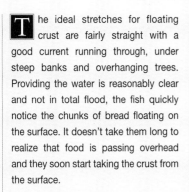

The ideal stretches for floating crust are fairly straight with a good current running through, under steep banks and overhanging trees. Providing the water is reasonably clear and not in total flood, the fish quickly notice the chunks of bread floating on the surface. It doesn't take them long to realize that food is passing overhead and they soon start taking the crust from the surface.

It is very important to use the right sort of bread: limp 'sliced white' is next to useless. Choose fresh baked white loaves, with tough thick crusts. It's about the most pleasant bait an angler ever has to handle and it works out a cheap hook and feed bait for a fishing session.

The tackle used for floating crust fishing is straightforward. The rod should be around twelve feet in order to control and mend line at distance. It needs to have enough backbone to set large hooks at range and to control a big chub in a strong current. Suitable rods are likely to be described as having a 'light specimen' or 'Avon' action, with test curves of about 1lb to 1¼ lb. Match rods are not really suitable: they have faster actions than required and will probably not be strong enough for this kind of fishing.

A good-quality fixed-spool reel is ideal for floating crust fishing. The main reel line would usually be four or five pounds test, to which the hook is tied direct. The line must not sink and get drowned: the last few metres should be greased with a fly fishing flotant if necessary.

Don't be afraid of using big hooks for this method. A chunk of crust the size of a matchbox is a big bait! I generally use sizes from two to six. Hook points must be needle sharp and the barbs as slender as possible, since they have to be drawn home on relatively light lines. Modern 'specimen' hooks with chemically etched points and 'whisker' barbs are excellent.

Having selected a suitable stretch of water, start by feeding the swim with a dozen pieces of bread, about the size of a ten-pence piece. Throw the crust well out into mid-stream and repeat this every minute until the fish start coming to the surface and taking the bread.

Watch out for fish that may be rising away off downstream. On a straight bit of river one can spot chub taking floating crust a hundred metres away. Once the fish really get the taste for crust they usually wolf it down, making big splashy rises. Now is the time to start fishing.

Get as close to the fish as possible, without scaring them. The less line there is lying on the surface, the less chance it will be caught by the current and pull the bait unnaturally off course. However enthusiastic they might appear, chub will quickly notice any false movement of the bait.

When a fish takes the baited hook, wait for the line to draw tight before striking. It needs a very deliberate strike, sweeping the rod back over one's head. If you strike too soon, you merely pluck the bait from between the fish's lips. The strike does need to be quite firm, since one is trying to set a large hook through a fairly tough bait. If you prick a fish, it will be badly spooked and further attempts in that spot will be a waste of time. Find a fresh stretch of river and start again.

LEFT: Touch legering is one of the most efficient ways of fishing barbel or chub river but it does demand a great deal of concentration. It is a huge advantage if you get into the water as this means that the distance between the angler and the bait — and hopefully the fish — is as short as possible. Line control is, therefore, easier and the bites are felt more easily. The second advantage of wading is that the angler really does become one with the river. The angler sitting on the bank never truly appreciates the subtleties of the current or the changes in water temperature. Good fishing is all about understanding fish and the greater amount of time the angler spends in the water with his quarry the more successful he is likely to be.

The river Ithon in central Wales. Early September. Generally clear weather but the odd shower brings down water temperatures minutely and occasionally adds a short-lived tinge of colour to the water. The promise of a warm day after a typically cool dawn with mist through the valley.

Chub are passionate about trees. Even a solitary overhanging tree along an otherwise featureless bit of river will attract most of the chub in that stretch. A tree offers a chub just about everything he needs in life. On a hot day, such as this, the dense foliage provides some relief from the sun. The leafy canopy screens the fish from winged predators flying overhead, while larger fish find some security among the tree roots against an otter attack. Otters are still relatively common in this isolated area of rural Wales and it is not unusual to find chub scales scattered on the bank like sad confetti after a dawn raid. Trees also provide chub with food and the species is noted for its fondness of windfalls such as caterpillars and beetles; even overripe elderberries and blackberries in their season.

ABOVE: Chub, including this impressive specimen, have huge mouths and can eat anything up to a large American signal crayfish in size. The throat-teeth of the chub are particularly powerful, designed to grind and crush the hardest shelled animals. Remember this and never be tempted to push out a deep hook with your finger. Chub have relatively large eyes and have the best eyesight of all fish. Even at night or in flood water chub can still pick out extremely small food items.

Actually, there doesn't seem to be very much that a chub will not eat and those great white lips can engulf most things from a drowning shrew to a passing frog or dace. Whatever passes down a chub's throat is crushed by powerful pharyngeal teeth that can pulp even a crayfish with ease.

Chips, popcorn and cherries are just a some of the unlikely baits that I've known to be successful for chub. However, when pursuing wild fish in an unspoiled river like the Ifon, natural baits make the best sense. All I have with me on this outing are a few worms and slugs. I know that if I run out of bait I can always grub out a few beetles or woodlice from under rocks or the bark of a dead tree, or find some little red worms beneath an old cow pat. There is always the chance, too, of finding a dead bullhead in the margins of the river or even a piece of rabbit flesh left by a fox. Chub will take just about anything, but, despite their huge appetites, they are far from easy to hook. Four hundred years ago, Izaak Walton called chub the 'fearfullest of fishes' and he was right.

The pool that I am now fishing is one of my old favourites and one that I visit first whenever I come to this part of the Ithon. It is situated just out of the town. In fact, the municipal bowling green is on the hillside above and one can hear the children in the school playground across the valley. At the head of the pool, the river runs under high rocky crags, then it opens out into a deep crystal pool, lined with trees. In places, the water is nine or ten feet deep, but the chub prefer the shallower margins where the branches overhang and the underwater roots sprawl. The sun is well up and I can see salmon parr darting about. A nice grayling holds itself in the faster current, just on the lip of the slower water.

Directly opposite me, under the branches of an alder tree, there is a very good chub indeed. In the bright sunlight I can see every detail: his scales; the rays of his fins; the roll of his eye and the white circle of his lips. He is holding position effortlessly, fins scarcely moving, his body simply pulsing slightly in the water. Every now and again he drifts a short way into the current to intercept a passing insect and his mouth opens with a gleam of white. As the morsel disappears, his eye rolls and I can sense how nearly a fish comes to satisfaction. His guard is never down, though. When a kingfisher spirits across the pool and lands on a branch a rod's length behind him, the fish sinks instantly from view.

Chub may not quite have eyes in the backs of their heads, but they give a pretty good impression of it! Certainly, their eyesight is acute and they seem to *notice* everything. After all, a chub uses its eyes as its first line of defence and for finding food and this it can do at night and in turbid flood water. In any event, this particular chub's eyesight seems in no way defective. Right now he is inspecting the lobworm I have just dropped towards him on the finest line I dare use in such a snag-infested swim. The hook is buried in the worm so nothing is visible. Surely I must stand a chance?

The approach is typical chub: a quick acceleration out of cover towards the worm that is falling naturally through the water. The fish stops abruptly a few inches from the worm, his pectorals beating, his eyes watching. As the worm sinks, the chub tips and follows it down, nose first. For just a moment I am sure he is about to take ... but no. The infuriating creature returns to the surface and glides back to his station under the branches. Those huge eyes must have spotted some tiny defect and the fish's innate wariness has saved him again.

But a chub like this does not survive on eyesight alone. A solitary crow flaps across the tail of the pool. Seeing me on the rocks, it croaks in alarm and in doing so drops a beetle that it had been carrying in its beak. The insect falls into the water several feet behind the fish. Instantly, the chub wheels round and is upon the struggling beetle in a flash. This time, there is no hesitation and the morsel disappears in a gulp.

With hearing and eyesight like this, the angler is hard pushed to fool large experienced chub. Indeed, there are occasions when we have to accept that some fish are practically uncatchable. If any fish can be described as 'wise', then this particular chub is about as clued up as they get and, on this occasion, I admit defeat. The best chance of hooking this fish would be in a winter flood perhaps, or on a dark moonless night when imperfections in presentation might go unnoticed. As for now, if I want to catch a fish at all, I must move on downriver searching the swims as I go.

Now I have arrived at a place where tangled willows and alders grow across the river. Fishing here is more like jungle warfare! I have to clamber over tree trunks and through seemingly impenetrable branches before I can even see the water. In such places, the chub seem to know that they are secure. It would be almost impossible to drop a bait to them

ABOVE: A very large chub has taken up station behind a fallen tree; you can just see the trailing branches at the edge of the picture. The fish knows that there is a hatch of fly present. In bright sunlight it has left the security of the roots and come up to the surface to take advantage of a plentiful food source. The chub is highly adaptable to circumstances and is, therefore, successful in many different types of water.

LEFT: This is a blast from the past, before fixed-spool reels, quivertips and swimfeeders were the norm in barbel fishing. Notice the centrepin reel and the float that led to the downfall of this lovely fish now wallowing in the shallows. Clive is wading out to the tiring barbel to slip the hook from the fish's lips with a pair of forceps. No need to net this fish, photograph it or weigh it; just let it get back to its home in mid-river as quickly as possible.

 through the latticework of foliage. At one point, however, I see three big fish right at the surface, close to the fringe of some weeping willows. By the cautious introduction of several slugs, I manage to entice one of the fish out into clear water where I might just be able to put a hooked bait to him. But these chub are also constantly wary. A girl on horseback fifty metres away calls out a greeting and canters off down the river bank. The three big fish sink from view and disappear for over an hour. The casual observer would never guess a single chub was present and yet this stretch of river is full of them.

I decide on a new approach. I pop into the town and come back with a loaf of fresh crusty bread. If there is one thing that chub like it is floating crust. For some reason, they simply adore it and it can be fished in the most straightforward of ways.

I choose a long, straight stretch of the river, with a steady push of current running under the inevitable trees. I break off a dozen chunks of crust from the loaf and toss them into mid-stream where they float off down towards haunts that I know are full of fish. The chub here have hardly ever seen floating crust. As far as I am aware, just I and a couple of friends ever use this method here and never more than twice in a season. Somehow, though, the chub seem to remember. Over the past ten years, we have caught perhaps a dozen or so fish from this river using floating crust. Nevertheless, it is almost uncanny how the word seems to get around.

Though I am sure that the chub want my pieces of bread, they are treated with great suspicion. One chub follows a piece of crust ten metres before coming up to suck it in. It knows that if the bread were attached to a line, at some point its drift would be false and unnatural.

Another chub, a really big one this time, comes slowly up to a piece of crust, gently sucks it down and then holds it between its lips for a full five minutes before swallowing it. It is almost as if the fish is waiting to see if there is a hook present. A strike by an impatient angler would simply pull it clear without any chance of hooking the fish.

A third fish watches a piece of crust very closely – obviously unsure about it. This chub's technique is dramatically different: it moves away from the crust, then turns and bats it sharply three or four times with its tail. The bread breaks into half a dozen pieces, some of which begin to sink. Only now does the chub spin round again and begin to pick off the fragments. It really is as if the fish *knew* that if a hook were present, it would have fallen out and now be lying useless on the river bed.

Whatever trick the angler devises, chub quickly develop some counter tactic, relying on their acute eyesight and extreme wariness. Moreover, one gets the distinct impression that they have incredibly long memories for distasteful experiences! On this occasion, I pack up fishless. Despite this, I have had a brilliant day. I've seen some fifty fish and put a bait near half of them. Half of those came so close I was sure they were going to take but, in the end, they all turned away.

Even a blank day like this has been bliss: reacquainting myself with a beautiful river and these extraordinarily cunning fish.

Chapter 2

Trout
The Art of Deception

IT WAS ONE EVENING BACK IN THE DAYS WHEN KASHMIR still enjoyed peace. The sun was setting, throwing violet lights onto the mountains from which a wonderful clear river streamed across the plain. Women were returning to the village with firewood on their backs. The menfolk were sitting around talking and spitting in the dust, while the boys of the village were fishing down by the bridge. Most were fishing with worms for bottom grubbing fish. One boy, about twelve years old, hunted down a moth and tied it to his bare hook with a strand of goat hair. With his crude tackle consisting of a long cane rod and a fixed line of a few feet of patched-together nylon, he lowered the bait onto the surface and let it float to a fish rising behind the bridge buttress. Up came a neb and the moth disappeared. As the nylon sprang tight, the thin cane bent, but the little Kashmiri boy held on and eventually beached the fish. 'A trout, Sahib!' he beamed. 'A trout!'. I had to take the fish from him, as he begged, or he would have fallen foul of the river keepers, who took their duties seriously in those days. Nevertheless, I recognized the pleasure on the boy's face. He had deceived a beautiful trout: almost everybody's favourite fish.

Globally, there are several related species that are called 'trout' by the anglers who fish for them. Biologically, they fall into three main categories: the brown trout (*Salmo trutta*) and its relatives of Eurasia; the rainbow trouts (*Oncorhynchus mykiss, et al*), related to the Pacific salmons

LEFT: Ever since the pattern set by Izaak Walton, anglers have loved not only to fish but also to teach fishing. Here a son receives sound guidance from his father – not that he needs a great deal: look how the rod is held instinctively high so that it can absorb the plunges of the struggling rainbow trout. Everything about the little boy's stance suggests confidence: he is standing straight, perfectly balanced, his gaze firmly on the fish, starting to anticipate what a hooked trout does when it feels the unaccustomed pressure of the bent rod.

and some of the chars (*Salvelinus* sp.), which occur around the holarctic. Every continent (except Antarctica) has its populations of 'trout'. Where they did not exist originally as indigenous species, they have been introduced by man and become well established. The family Salmonidae is notoriously difficult to classify and has presented taxonomists with a headache, even with the very latest genetic techniques. Taken as a whole, *all* 'trout' are beautiful game fish and, of whichever species, they are prized by anglers the world over.

The art of deceiving a trout into mistaking a creation of fur and feather for a real insect has origins lost way back in history. The Roman writer, Claudius Aelianus, gave a recognizable account of fly fishing in Macedonia in the third century, while detailed instructions are to be found in the famous *Treatyse on Fysshynge Wyth an Angle* (1496), attributed to Dame Juliana Berners, Abbess of Sopwell. Fly fishing really took off in England in the nineteenth century, when a succession of pioneering anglers sought to tie flies that could fool the fastidious brown trout of the crystal chalk streams of Wessex. These fishers were the first of the 'angler entomologists', who carried to new levels the study of the insects upon which the trout fed. Men like Ronalds, Marryat, Halford and Skues shaped the art of fly fishing into the sport as we have it today.

One conjures up visions of that Golden Age of fly fishing: of leisured Victorian gentlemen in Norfolk jackets and knickerbockers chasing round the water meadows with butterfly nets, collecting specimens for examination under the microscope. The stomach contents of trout caught were analyzed and catalogued with meticulous care and, season after season, knowledge was built up about the feeding habits of the fish. At the same time, these anglers strove to tie increasingly close representations of the natural insects.

Then, as now, the golden period on every chalk stream was the few days in early summer when the exquisite mayfly appears. For the magic two weeks of the mayfly hatch, the Duffer's Fortnight as it was known, anglers would make their excuses domestically and professionally and catch the train from Waterloo down to Hampshire. Despite popular myth, the occurrence of the mayfly hatch is not absolutely precise. It may be shifted backwards or forwards, depending on the spring weather of the particular year and on the location of the river. Southern rivers are generally 'earlier' than Northern rivers, for example. When the vast swarms of these large, succulent insects emerge, the trout (and just about everything else) devour them in a huge delirious feast. It is a time when the biggest and most cautious fish may drop their guard and be deceived by the angler's fly.

The River Test in early June. A mild day with a brisk wind and high cloud cover. Charles Jardine takes up the quest to tie the perfect mayfly imitation and catch that fish of a lifetime.

Mayflies rise in spiralling flight from the water, their gauzy wings glowing in the sunlight. The flies fill the Test valley like a snowstorm and the trout are gorging on them. As far as the eye can see the river's surface is disturbed by the swirls of rising fish, some even leaping into the air occasionally to take the succulent insects in flight. This is gluttony. It is one of the few times when the normally wary chalk stream fish are on the rampage, throwing their innate caution to the winds.

Despite its brief season, the mayfly has an inordinate importance in the valley. Even the inn two miles upstream is named after it. And trout are not the only creatures that feed on them. Swans gorge on them, scooping them from the surface and dipping their long necks below the surface in search of the rising nymphs. A hobby – that rare and tiny falcon – rises and stoops for the flying insects: an extraordinary sight. It is just one of many birds taking them in flight. In the river, roach are sipping in the nymphs, while dace, chub and grayling contribute to the surface commotion. Even eels snake up from the bottom to gulp down the nymphs and emerging duns. Toads feed on the bodies of the spent flies that drift into the margins, whilst bats take over the aerial attack at dusk. Even an owl keeps an eye open for a stray or two as he courses the water meadows.

The positions in a river, where trout more or less permanently station themselves, are known as 'lies'. A lie is of governing importance to a trout. It provides the fish with comfort, security and a larder. A good lie will always be found where the current brings a steady procession of food items past the resident's nose. Once a fish has found a good lie, he rarely strays far from it. It becomes his base camp. There is a pecking order in the river, though, and the biggest fish will occupy the best lies. These are defended vigorously against intruders. Even a three-pound

ABOVE: *The real mayfly is positioned close to the paints while Charles Jardine sketches it onto his pad. This exercise forces Charles to study carefully every detail of the fly. He is trying to understand exactly what the trout sees when it looks at the mayfly so that he knows which features he has to imitate when it comes to tying the fly.*

RIGHT: *The angler who can tie his own flies is at a distinct advantage, especially when there's no tackle shop close by. If you can't tie flies, nothing is more frustrating than losing the one pattern that seems to be working on the day. More than that, the ability to tie flies allows the angler to copy anything unusual that might be hatching at that particular time. Trout can be highly discriminating and, if the angler does not have the exact imitation to tie to the end of his line, he is likely to go home fishless.*

An ongoing challenge for the trout angler is to discover on which insects the trout are feeding at any particular time. The correct imitation can then be used and the chances of catching a fish are much higher. Often, although it is not possible to see what kind of insects or flies the trout are taking, the way in which the trout are feeding gives out clear messages. This is fishing detective work at its highest level and demands that the angler observes the fish closely, interprets its behaviour correctly and finally fishes in the most appropriate manner.

The trout's primary consideration when feeding is that it does not waste energy and it will move quickly only when necessary. This means that a feeding fish is swift only when trying to eat something that is itself quick and vigorous. When taking a water snail, for example, the trout moves slowly and so, it can be seen, there is a direct relationship between the speed of the fish and the creature it is trying to catch and consume. This behaviour is demonstrated by the water itself because a fast-moving trout displaces the water around it forcibly and makes a very obvious boil or splash on the surface. A slow-moving trout displaces water much more gently and its feeding patterns are therefore more difficult to detect. Let's look at some examples.

Large swirls just below the surface that do not break the film of the water are made by trout moving quickly near the surface, chasing fast-moving nymphs or pupae a few inches down. Sedges, midges and olives are all possible victims too. If the trout is vigorously splashing through the film then its targets are much more likely to be large, fast-moving insects such as adult sedges. The momentum of the avidly hunting trout carries it up and through the surface film, creating the splash that the angler can see and interpret.

Sometimes the trout moves very gently on the surface revealing its back, tail and nose; this is typical trout behaviour when taking smaller duns or even flies blown onto the water from the bank. When the trout behaves like this but its mouth does not break the surface, then it is hunting small insect forms trapped within the surface film or trying to struggle through it. A perfect example of such creatures, especially on lakes, are midge pupae waiting to hatch.

When a breeze is throwing up a ripple on the water's surface, the angler may see a smooth patch, like a small oil slick, appear for no apparent reason. This is produced by a trout turning violently on a nymph some way down and pushing water up to the surface which calms the ripple for a short while. Conversely, in calm water reflections may occasionally 'bend' a little as a trout turns when feeding beneath the surface and pushes up a boil of water that contorts the surface film.

Sound, too, can be useful when determining what trout are feeding on. If, for example, the angler hears a sipping noise accompanied by only a little surface displacement then the trout is almost certainly moving slowly to take dead or dying insects off the surface. The noise is made by the trout's mouth opening and sucking in air. The trout creates little splash because it knows that the insect cannot escape.

chub is not safe from the teeth of an eight-pound brown and woe betide the minnow, gudgeon or dace that passes too close. And, of course, the choicest lies are invariably the ones that the fisherman finds impossible to put a fly over! The best fish seem to have a knack of finding the best protected lies. They are always under some overhanging branch, a protruding tree root or a nasty little eddy in the current that spoils the presentation of the fly. The lies of big fish become legendary along the river and local experts will discuss various ways a fly may be cast to them. They almost inevitably fail!

To fishermen, like Jardine, who dream of catching extraordinary trout, the mayfly brings opportunity, for it can tempt the biggest, wisest fish out of their lies. And, once out of their lies, these crafty old fish are suddenly vulnerable. Even the wariest trout let their guards down, intoxicated by the irresistible glut of food raining down around them. Temptation grows slowly to start with. At first, only the smaller fish succumb. Then, as the hatch progresses, the larger and warier fish become infected by the feeding frenzy and join the mêlée. At last, the biggest browns join in. Their feeding is still more deliberate and cautious than that of their more impetuous younger brethren, but when the mayfly are at their height, they do so with greater abandon than at most other times in the year.

Unlike the younger trout which snatch the flies from the surface, the older trout sidle up to the hapless insects and consider them carefully before slurping them down. Spent or crippled flies are preferred, since they are completely trapped in the surface film and cannot escape. They allow the closest scrutiny and offer the easiest meals.

It is here on a beautiful beat of the Test, halfway into the mayfly carnival, that the paths of one particular big brown trout and Charles Jardine are soon to cross. Charles is in the finest tradition of a fly angler. In the spirit of Halford and Skues he seeks to tie the best possible imitation and present it as faultlessly as possible, to the largest and most difficult fish in the river. To anglers like these, this is the quintessential challenge.

But there is work to be done before Charles can even consider casting to the fish. On this occasion, none of the artificials in his fly box had met with his approval. While many of them had proved their worth in the past, today they seemed to lack a certain something. None of the

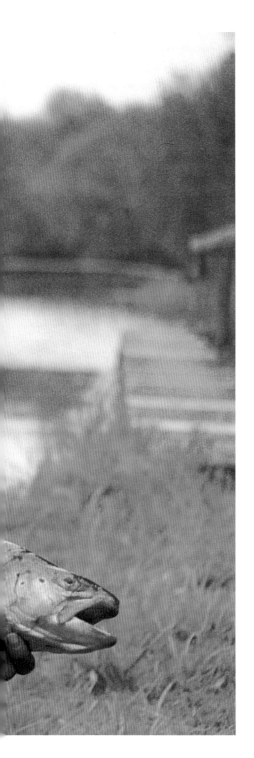

LEFT: *This is a very fine brown trout indeed, a real monster. Its tremendous bulk has been built up by weeks of rich feeding during the mayfly season. Brown trout have a remarkable ability to adapt to their environment and trout from a poor, acidic mountain stream would be very different in shape and colouring.*

ABOVE: *This tiny upland brown trout is a fully formed mature fish; the background of mosses and mountain wild flowers help to explain its small size. Moorland streams and tarns are very poor in insect life, and during the summer months many fish exist almost solely on terrestrial insects blown from the moor by strong winds. Size, of course, is not everything and it is impossible to imagine a more vividly coloured trout or one better suited to its environment.*

serried ranks of fur and feather had inspired him with confidence. And confidence in one's fly is everything in this game!

The morning has broken mild and Charles is down on the river catching mayflies for closer study. Some he snatches out of the air, but he is particularly interested in those he finds on the water's surface. Today he has decided to concentrate on the spent mayfly: the female insect that has shed her eggs and is floating downstream, dead or dying, trapped in the surface film. It is this spent condition that he wants to study carefully to see if he can imitate it.

He catches the insect he is looking for and settles down with his brush and little box of watercolours to paint the features he is interested in. Charles is a professional artist and he uses his sketchpad as a pictorial notebook. The body and wings are of course noticeable, but Charles makes special note of the splayed and helpless legs of the insect. Exactly what the trout sees and how this translates to its brain is something we will never be certain of. However, years of highly successful fishing have given Charles more than a few clues. He is sure that the pattern of the legs and the feet on the surface is an important trigger to the fish's feeding response.

Charles puts the fly in a jam jar filled with water and turns it round against the light, looking at the patterns made on the surface by the feebly struggling insect. For several minutes, the artist studies the insect, trying hard to imagine how a brown trout would see it. Once again, it is that 'footprint' of indentations in the surface film that he finds distinctive. Only after he has given the creature the minutest examination does he feel ready to attempt an imitation.

In a quiet corner of the Mayfly Inn, Charles assembles his fly-tying gear. To the uninitiated this is an arcane business and the table is soon strewn with gorgeous feathers and furs; strange-looking instruments and mysterious little packets and pouches. This is alchemy, make no mistake, for here the fly tier tries to recreate the living insect. A mere facsimile is not enough: he must attempt to imbue it with life.

With the painting of the mayfly before him and the natural insect still in the jar, Charles sets about tying an imitation that might succeed where previous attempts have failed. He has decided to tie the fly a little larger than life size, reasoning that a 'super meal' – if not overdone – will be a bigger temptation for a greedy fish. Above all, he is going to try and recreate that footprint pattern on the surface. He is convinced that this is crucial, since this is the first thing a trout sees of an approaching meal. All the while as he ties, he refers back constantly to the natural insect in the jar and to his sketchpad of painted notes.

The fabricated insect grows in the vice, a creation of moose tail, hare fur and silks. As he ties, Charles is transported mentally to the waters of the Test flowing outside the window. 'Just what will this thing look like to that big old trout? Have I stresssed the right features? Will it be enough to deceive him?' Only time will tell.

Down on the river, the day has grown overcast. The hatch is perfect for the fisherman. Mayflies are trickling past steadily, but not too abundantly. Too many insects and the trout either become completely sated, or the angler's artificial can hardly be noticed, lost amongst the multitude.

Smaller fish are everywhere, cartwheeling after the flies and bow-waving after the rising nymphs in their eagerness. Charles is not interested in these fish. He is in no hurry and his careful observation of the water is deceptively casual as he walks slowly upstream. He is after just one particular fish today ... no other. There is a brisk wind blowing downstream and this weakens the water's surface film, allowing the flies to break through and rise off quickly. The trout have to be a little sharper now if they are to catch the insects before they escape. This is not how the big brown trout wants to operate and Charles knows it. He continues slowly upriver until, on a bend, he finds the sort of area he has been searching for. On the far side, the river is sheltered by a high bank and the water is calmer. Here the surface is less ruffled and it will be harder for insects to break free from the surface tension. Big, experienced fish know instinctively that in patches of water like this they will have easier pickings and more time to inspect their prey.

Charles settles down to watch, his silhouette masked by a tree. It is not long before his trained eye spots something. This is what he is after: a large mahogany-brown head breaks the surface as a big fish rolls lazily, picking off an easy meal. Charles watches him for a further five or ten minutes, plotting exactly where he is going to place his fly. Now it is a matter of getting into position without causing alarm and Charles half crawls to the river bank, his eyes never leaving the fish. The fly is tied onto the leader and the rod waves rhythmically, to and fro in the

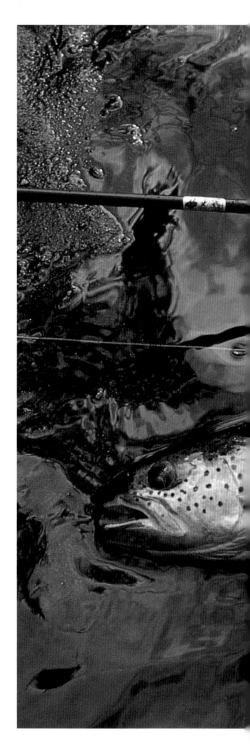

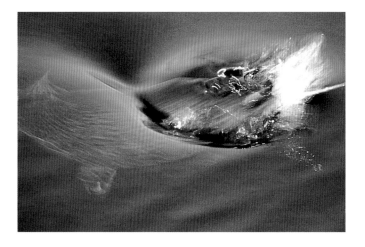

ABOVE: The water surface explodes as a trout slashes for a mayfly. The larger and more quickly moving the fly, the faster the hunting fish has to strike. This is no delicate, easily paced sip from the surface but a full-blooded dash at a large, juicy meal which is about to lift off into the air and safety.

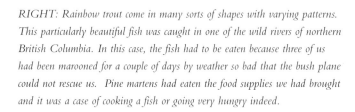

RIGHT: Rainbow trout come in many sorts of shapes with varying patterns. This particularly beautiful fish was caught in one of the wild rivers of northern British Columbia. In this case, the fish had to be eaten because three of us had been marooned for a couple of days by weather so bad that the bush plane could not rescue us. Pine martens had eaten the food supplies we had brought and it was a case of cooking a fish or going very hungry indeed.

 afternoon light, as an expert caster finds his range. Satisfied that the length is right, Charles makes his delivery.

With the tiniest plop, the fly falls perhaps a creel's length in front of the fish's nose. The big brown sees the fly and the faint vibrations radiating from its minute collision with the water give the desired impression of life. The dimpled imprint on the surface conveys the suggestion of insect legs and the deception is clinched. For the first and last time in perhaps six long years, a big brown trout makes its only mistake.

It is June on the River Lyd in Devon. David Pilkington, of the Arundel Arms, is sitting by the Mar Lodge Pool. The river is low and clear, but the night is warm and overcast. He knows it is a good sea trout night.

Sea trout fishing on a summer's night. The very thought of it evokes some of the most haunting images in fishing. Twilight is giving way to darkness when the big silver fish begin to move. If trout are the world's favourite angling fish, then the sea trout is even more special. They are the same species as brown trout, biologically, but their life cycles and behaviour are quite different.

The early life of a sea trout is similar to that of Atlantic salmon. It spends its first two or three years in the river, going through the stages of alevin, fry and parr until it finally dons the silver coat of a smolt and migrates downriver to the sea. It is here that the sea trout's story grows indistinct. Some sea trout probably travel little further than the estuaries of their native rivers, but others are true wanderers and are sometimes caught by fishing vessels on the high seas. Some fish certainly run hundreds of miles looking for feeding grounds. Tagging has shown that Tweed fish, for example, visit the Norfolk coastline throughout the summer to gorge on the sand eel, shrimps, peeler crabs, lugworms and sprats that flourish in the warm shallow water. Sometime in the summer months, the silvery sea trout feel the call to return to the rivers of their birth to breed.

Here on the Mar Lodge Pool, David Pilkington has noticed one particular fish that is unusually big for a Devon river. She has been lying quietly, resting on the bottom of the deep pool: easily the largest fish in the shoal around her. Unlike a big river brown trout, this fish is not territorial. Like salmon, adult sea trout do not feed in fresh water and there is no competition for food. Nevertheless, the best lies will still be chosen by the biggest fish. Mar Lodge is an ideal halt for a run of sea trout to rest in. The water is deep and overhung by trees, giving protection from the blazing summer sun.

As evening closes in and the sun sinks behind the trees on the bank opposite, the fish begin to mill around the pool. Some of them will press on further upstream tonight. Even in low water conditions sea trout find it hard not to run. Some of the fish still have sea lice on their bodies, which means that they may have covered the thirty miles from the sea in just a couple of nights. There are few more magical sights in angling than to watch a run of sea trout pushing up through shallow water under the light of the moon. On occasions they come up through water so shallow that it barely covers the stones, let alone their muscular backs. As they thrash their tails violently to drive themselves over the stickles, the sound of it can be heard a hundred metres off in the quietness of the night.

The big four-pound sea trout has been in the river for a week and in that particular pool for four or five days. She seems in no hurry to leave. Each evening, after the bats have started to flit about and the red deer have come down into the potato field to feed, she swims slowly around the pool in leisurely exploration of her territory.

As usual, David Pilkington arrives in the last of the light to assemble his tackle. His gear ready, he sits down and waits, acclimatizing himself to the falling darkness and the tune of the river. There is a heronry in the wood behind and the young have hatched. Throughout the night the adult birds will be coming and going, sometimes croaking in alarm the few times they see his torchlight or hear his boot splash in the water. The first fish are beginning to jump and David knows that the sea trout are becoming active, but he still waits until the green has gone out of the grass and all has become monochrome around him.

Now it is dark enough and David starts, cautiously crouching on the exposed gravel bar. He has to be really careful here, since any flagrant movement will be seen. He knows that sea trout are extremely shy, as many anglers discover to their cost. Disturb even one fish and the whole shoal is unnerved, ready to depart should the threat increase. David fishes to a pattern, fanning short casts around him so that all the nearby water is covered. He then increases the length of his casts, gradually extending

RIGHT: *As the moon begins to shine through the water, the sea trout, that has been sheltering under weed and rocks all day, begins to move, sniff the current and think about its upstream migration. This fish, its eye rolling round the socket, its fins beginning to move, is preparing itself for the rigours of the night.*

the area his flies are searching. His retrieve is slow and rhythmic. He compares it with stroking a cat. All is executed faultlessly in the velvety darkness, by touch and instinct born of long experience. Despite the clear water and the moon starting to emerge, it is doubtful whether the sea trout can see a fly from more than a couple of feet away.

Working slowly along the gravel bar David continues his diligent search of the pool with short and long casts radiating from each stance. On one cast, he drops his large black fly just inches from the fronds of an overhanging fern. He lets the lure sink a moment, knowing that the water under that bank is deep. At the first pull of his retrieve, it is taken solidly by what is obviously a big fish.

Immediately, she runs towards David, who cannot maintain contact. Beaching herself momentarily in her panic, she kicks up the water and splashes the angler in the face. Ricocheting back into the sanctuary of the pool, the fish careers around and jumps three times. But she is starting to tire and keels over briefly onto her side. She summons up the energy for another run and, suddenly ... the hook falls out! With a sigh, David wishes her good luck. He knows from long experience that such things happen all too frequently in sea trout fishing. Nonetheless, his pulse is racing. Even after years of fishing, such explosive fights on a still

ABOVE: A good sea trout is pulled into the net, its mouth agape and its strength spent. The black fly responsible for the catch can be seen in the trout's top jaw. The luminous specks around the trout are insects illuminated by a flash gun.

The late Hugh Falkus probably understood sea trout better than any other angler in history and he was constantly aware that to catch them consistently at night the fisherman had to tune in with their changing moods. Hugh defined three main taking periods: the 'first half' that runs roughly from dusk until around midnight. 'Half time' he described as lasting from half-past midnight to around 1.30 a.m. whilst the 'second half' is played out between 1.30 a.m. and daybreak. He also called the period of sunrise 'extra time', the occasional extension of the game when sea trout can still be taken.

It is in this 'first half' when the sea trout are at their most active, shaking off the lethargy of the day and exploring the pool, looking for new lies and often pushing up the runs into the pools above. Energy levels are high and the fish will take a fly that is drawn back fairly quickly through the surface layers. Falkus himself recommended a 'medicine' type lure, a slimly dressed fly on a size 4 hook, predominantly blue and silver in colour and intended to simulate a small, escaping fish. This is dynamic fishing; the trout are active and excitable at this time of night. However, near midnight, the scene begins to change.

During the period around 1.00 a.m. the sea trout start to move deeper into the water, most of their journeying and exploration now over. New lies have been scouted out and are being taken up and it's easy to think that the trout are no longer willing to accept a fly. This is not the case: it is simply that they have to be pursued at a deeper level. A sunk lure is now more appropriate and depending on the depth of the pool, a sinking line. The lure must be fished more slowly too, meticulously searching out any sea trout still willing to make a mistake. This is calmer, more controlled fishing and the pools have to be worked far more steadily. However, fish are unpredictable and just occasionally it pays to pull a large surface lure quickly across the surface, especially towards the tail of the pool – a tactic that can rise a fish from the bottom and induce a slashing take.

Falkus himself was always a stickler for staying out a little bit longer until the sun had actually appeared on the horizon. At this point, sparsely dressed flies fished on a floating line close to the surface may arouse the interest of the fish once again. This may be because a few late-night travellers have arrived in the pool and are still searching out suitable lies.

Things are changing, however, in the sea trout world. An increasing number of anglers today will not only stay on for the first hour of sunrise but know that sea trout can be caught during the day. The daytime sea trout is easily spooked though and the approach has to be especially cautious. Flies must be small; tiny, dry flies tied on a size 16 will often raise big fish to the surface in a slow but determined rise.

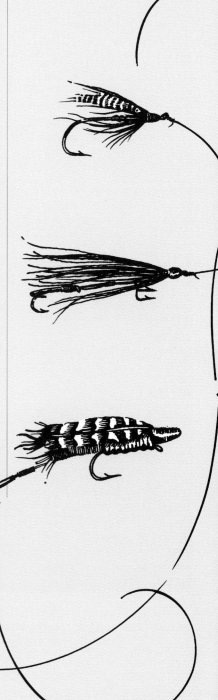

summer's night never cease to thrill him. But the story is not yet done.

Two nights later, in exactly the same position and in similar conditions, David is back at the Mar Lodge Pool. The moon shows through high, even cloud. In the faint light he has just made out the disturbance of a large rise in an eddy, some fifteen metres downstream of the gravel. It is clearly a good fish and he starts his cautious and methodical approach.

On just his second cast, David's gently worked fly is taken without hesitation. For a second time on that pool in as many days, the angler finds himself connected to a big sea trout crashing about in the darkness. Wildly it fights, making for all the snags in the pool. At almost any time in the first five minutes, the fish could have been lost. At last, her strength goes, she turns on her side and the angler is able to draw her over the stones in the shallows.

She is a terrific fish for the river, but surely it would be too great a coincidence to have two sea trout of such size in the same pool in so short a time? As he unhooks her, his suspicions are confirmed. There, in her jaw, is a second mark. It is the wound where the same fly had penetrated forty-eight hours before. The fish had beaten him then, but now he is the victor. With honours even it seems only fair to call it quits. Gently righting the fish, he holds her in the shallow water for a few moments to recover. Then, with a quick thrust of her tail, she disappears into the darkness.

After her scare, the sea trout had decided to move position, but for some reason seemed unwilling to vacate the pool. She had been so long in the river that she had started to take the occasional sedges and caddis pupae, despite her supposed fast. In the ocean, sea trout are aggressive feeders, their lives dominated by the search for food. However, like salmon, on their return to the river to spawn, the sea trout stop feeding to all intents and purposes. The occasional morsel that is taken from time to time probably has more to do with a reflex reaction to a feeding stimulus, than any genuine desire to feed. This is all the angler can rely on and his lure has to be presented just right to trigger the response.

Chapter 3

Carp
The Wariest of Fish

IN BRITAIN, MORE PEOPLE FISH FOR CARP THAN FOR ANY other species because of their size, their power and their undoubted beauty. Above all, anglers like the challenge of carp because they are so very wary and cunning. Even in their 'wild' state, in waters that are hardly fished, carp show the deepest suspicion of anything unusual. In lakes subjected to angling pressure, however, carp quickly become wise to the angler's ploys and seem to have an uncanny ability to get the measure of any new tricks within a very short time.

Mid-June in Wiltshire and Chris Yates is preparing to fish a lovely and secluded five-acre lake on a private estate. The weather is hot and still, with the slight threat of a storm during the night. Chris reckons that the fish are most likely to be moving and feeding in the evening and again at dawn.

The name Chris Yates is held in awe by carp anglers. This is not simply because be held the British record for over a decade with a marvellous fish well over fifty pounds. He is admired, as much, because he does his own thing and ploughs a very independent lone furrow through the increasingly frenetic and fashion-governed world of carp fishing. Chris learned his craft when the sport was a simpler and more direct affair. In those days, the angler was more concerned with the fish than with vastly sophisticated tackle, rigs or baits. As far as Chris is concerned, there is only one way to catch carp and that is to get to know the fish intimately. One has to learn their habits and even the whims and idiosyncrasies of individual fish. After years of minute observation, Chris Yates is a carp fishing genius.

This lake in the forest is the sort of water Chris has dreamed of since childhood. It is totally unspoiled, very old and achingly beautiful and

LEFT: It would be hard to find a more contented human being. The kettle is steaming, the tea is warm and comforting and the sun is just beginning to set over the stirring carp lake. Bliss.

Chris has no intention of allowing his presence to mar the scene. He blends in effortlessly with the forest around him, which is now afire with rays from the setting sun. Chris has no tent, though he intends staying all night. An ordinary black umbrella will have to do if there is a storm and he will light only a small fire for his kettle. His gear is minimalist, for this is how he likes to fish: merging into the bankside undergrowth with the least possible intrusion.

Only Chris and half-a-dozen or so friends have permission to fish here and it is their unwritten rule to go elsewhere if anyone is already fishing the lake. This means that the lake is never fished by more than one angler at a time and the carp may not see an angler's bait for days or even weeks on end. These carp are subjected to hardly any pressure and their behaviour is as natural as can be.

Chris moves cautiously through the wood dappled by the afternoon sunshine. A careless foot snapping a fallen branch could spell disaster for his fishing. He uses the cover of trees and bushes like a hunter, which is what, of course, he is. His coat and hat are drab and dun coloured and even his dark beard helps his camouflage. Carp like these have an almost unreal ability to sense when their environment is being invaded by an unwelcome alien. Many modern anglers visiting such a pristine water would ruin their chances before even setting up a rod.

Carp that grow very old and large, reinforce their instincts and innate faculties by learning. This is not in the intellectual sense that humans learn, but they are capable of registering experience and acquiring a store of responses to these experiences. If any fish can be described as intelligent, then big old carp are the first contenders. These fish lead relatively ordered existences, with only the seasonal and climatic changes in their environment. Anything out of the ordinary will be noticed and even when the fish seem totally preoccupied with feeding, they are constantly alert. And, like many other creatures, carp have the ability to communicate unease or fear. This needn't involve surging off in panicked flight. Carp seem perfectly capable of transmitting signals to other carp by the subtlest of body language, undiscernible to any but other carp and certainly not to the angler.

In the warm sunshine of late afternoon the carp of the lake are resting and at their most infuriating. They have been basking for twelve hours now, lying in the milk-warm water with their bellies caressed by beds of soft weed. They give every impression of contentment. Stalking carefully, Chris can get so close to these fish that he can see their eyes roll and the languid movements of their fins. These are definitely not feeding fish and are almost impossible to catch in this condition. They are simply not interested in anything but relaxing in the sunshine. Occasionally, however, the sun will get too much for them and they will drift away into the shade of overhanging trees. It is there, in the cool and particularly as evening approaches, that the occasional fish will decide to look for a snack.

Chris spends a couple of hours just watching, looking for any sign of a fish bubbling or clouding the water. It takes him all that time to move slowly and cautiously around the lake, but he doesn't see a single fish that looks as though it might take a bait. Returning to his base, he brews a welcome cup of tea and enjoys the last of the sunshine before darkness falls. As the dusk begins to creep over the water he decides to turn in for the night and get some sleep. Tomorrow will be an early start.

The first light of dawn filters through the trees showing Chris still asleep, curled up between the roots of an ancient tree. He has no difficulty sleeping rough like this. With dew on his coat and a spider's web glistening on the rim of his hat he looks like a dishevelled tramp. There are not many who would relish spending the night like this, but by doing so, Chris is in position and absolutely ready to fish. He has even avoided the possibility that an approach down through the meadow in daylight might have alarmed the lake's wary residents.

Chris is woken by the sunlight shining on his face. He gets up and stretches cautiously, screened from the water by a rhododendron bush, and lights a fire for his kettle. As he drinks his tea, he sits and takes in what is happening around the lake. Soon he is on the move. He has decided to move round the lake to the west bank. He wants to try a slight promontory, covered by thick trees that will give him cover. Changing pitch like this is easy for Chris: he has only one rod and a small bag to carry. Even his rod-rest is simply the traditional forked stick, which he whittled from a branch of a fallen tree the previous evening. The early sun warms him up and the exercise works out any remaining stiffness from his night under the tree. He is not the only creature to appreciate the sun's rays. The lake's biggest carp have also moved over to the west bank, where the water is now just a half degree warmer than those

RIGHT: *This is a carp at peace with the world. The water at the surface is both calm and warm and, in conditions such as these, carp love to drift aimlessly in the late afternoon, enjoying the caressing sensation of the water on their bodies. When relaxed, carp stretch their dorsal fins languidly, gently breaking the surface of the water.*

LEFT: Here is the perfect carp lake, set in a secluded spot in forest and protected from the winds. A layer of surface scum has built up in the bays in the background of the picture – the ideal place for a browsing carp to suck in fallen insects and stray moths. Carp activity can be seen at the left of the picture – a large fish stirring beneath the surface as it hoovers up mouthfuls of daphnia. This is an old, rich lake and it is no wonder that the carp do so well here.

areas still in shade. A glorious, golden mist rises swirling from the lake's surface and beneath it Chris can see trails of bubbles sent up by feeding fish. Occasionally, the tip of a fin breaks the surface in the shallow water.

The very best carp lakes are ancient. Whilst almost all of them were originally man-made, their very age confers on them a naturalness and even, almost, a touch of magic. Both the lake and its carp are mysterious and venerable: the one making the perfect setting for the other. This particular water is perhaps a thousand years old and was once used as a stew pond for the castle that still stands in the next valley. Around its banks lie the ruins of ancient masonry, testimony to structures erected and decayed over the centuries. Records show that Oliver Cromwell fished the lake in the seventeenth century and, tyrant that he was, killed every fish that he caught there.

Age has brought immense richness to the water, for the centuries have laid a thick bed of silt on the lake bed. The ooze on the bottom is home to huge colonies of bloodworm, the tiny red midge larvae that carp love to 'hoover' up. The fish are doing exactly this now and moving gradually towards the bank where Chris is standing watching them.

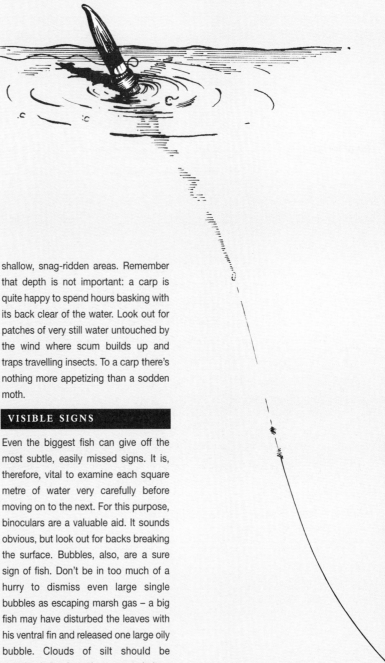

A s much care as possible must be taken when stalking carp. Think about the clothing you wear. Clothes should be drab to blend in with the surroundings and loose to disguise body shape. An extra layer of thorn-proof clothing is wise as nettles and thistles can prove a hazard. A hat is also a good idea, both to cast shade over the face and to keep glare off it in sunlight. Polaroid glasses are absolutely essential and, when fishing early or late in the day and around marshy areas, insect repellent is very useful.

Consider your footwear: plimsolls or trainers are excellent if there is a lot of dead undergrowth around but thigh boots or even chest-waders may be preferable if there is a chance that you need to go into the water for a snagged fish.

LOCATION

To stalk successfully you need to find a quiet bank, well away from the usual crowd of anglers. Unfortunately these will probably be in areas where it is difficult to present baits comfortably. The banks in such an area will often be tree-lined with lots of fallen bushes, branches and underwater snags. Islands just off the banks are good locations too and lilybeds and channels are well worth investigating. Carp use all of these areas for sanctuary, to escape from the general hubbub of the lake and enjoy the feeling of security afforded by the quiet surroundings. There is usually a great deal of natural food in these shallow, snag-ridden areas. Remember that depth is not important: a carp is quite happy to spend hours basking with its back clear of the water. Look out for patches of very still water untouched by the wind where scum builds up and traps travelling insects. To a carp there's nothing more appetizing than a sodden moth.

VISIBLE SIGNS

Even the biggest fish can give off the most subtle, easily missed signs. It is, therefore, vital to examine each square metre of water very carefully before moving on to the next. For this purpose, binoculars are a valuable aid. It sounds obvious, but look out for backs breaking the surface. Bubbles, also, are a sure sign of fish. Don't be in too much of a hurry to dismiss even large single bubbles as escaping marsh gas – a big fish may have disturbed the leaves with his ventral fin and released one large oily bubble. Clouds of silt should be examined closely as they are an obvious

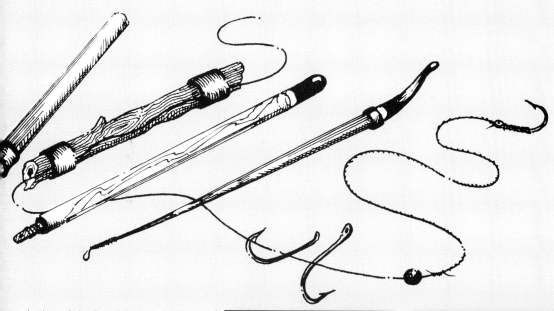

sign of feeding fish and a sudden 'welling' on the water surface indicates fish on the move. This is hard to describe but look out for the water rising and falling in a very gentle manner as it is displaced by fish moving through it. When you see a fish, weigh up the chances of landing it. Don't be irresponsible and, if the carp is completely entrenched, then pass it by.

THE TOOLS

A short and powerful rod is essential for stalking. Long rods get caught up in the branches of trees and are difficult to make a swing cast with. A centrepin reel is a good idea as it allows you to be in direct contact with the fish immediately but a fixed-spool reel can be useful too. Take great care with your line choice: using a twelve or fifteen pound line is not excessive. Check it again and again for any sign of abrasion or weakness, especially after you have landed a fish. And, lastly, a strong arm is needed to hustle big fish out into open water.

END TACKLE

For this type of fishing a float is almost essential but, do be careful, the fish will be aware of any float that is too large for the job. If fish show any signs of caution, think again about your choice of float and perhaps move on to a transparent-bodied float. If you are still having problems try a natural float. A quill or a piece of twig cannot be beaten if long casting is not necessary. Try lying your float or quill on the surface rather than having it cocked as often in shallow water a carp may come across the stem of the cocked float and be frightened away.

Braided line can be useful for stalking, for example a camouflaged braid might overcome any remaining doubts a very wary fish may have. Hooks should be as strong as possible. Holding a big fish in a confined space puts an enormous amount of strain on the tackle and a suspect hook will bend like Plasticine.

BAIT

This is the perfect opportunity to experiment with different natural baits. Lobworms are the most effective as they wriggle vigorously and, in so doing, attract the carp's attention. Wasp grubs are excellent bait if you can get hold of them. Other baits which give very good results are caterpillars, a big bunch of brandlings or slugs, which you can catch at dawn from flowerbeds or from a vegetable patch. Try tethering a large drowned moth on the bottom – carp find these irresistible.

Other particles such as casters, maggots or sweet corn can be used. Hair-rigging baits are not necessary as the carp feels relatively secure and should suck in the hook and bait with confidence.

RIGHT: The quieter the water, the more alarmed the carp is by human presence. Carp are often easier to stalk where there is some bank-side disturbance. Therefore, when fishing a peaceful area of water like this camouflage is all important. Chris Yates knows this and stands, facing the dawn, in clothing that blends into the background perfectly. Only his face stands out brightly and even that is half covered with his beard!

Preoccupied with their feeding, the fish upend and thrust their snouts sometimes inches down into the mud as they rummage about. Here and there the tails of big fish wave clear of the surface, glinting a second like wet flags in the sun. As they feed greedily, the huge fish stir up the mud and the water becomes increasingly turbid.

In rich waters like this, the carp's diet consists almost entirely of small invertebrates: bloodworm, daphnia, shrimps, beetles and tiny snails. The whole lake is a larder, heaving with juicy titbits. Unlike the fish in relatively barren, newly created angling lakes, these fish have no need of anglers' baits for sustenance and neither have they been educated to take them. Carp like these are quite different creatures to the imported roly-poly European fish that are stocked into newly dug pits.

The fish that Chris watches now are the descendants of carp that have been in the lake for centuries. They are sleek and powerful, but of leaner proportions than the 'fatties' produced by the modern fish breeder. Their muscular bodies, large fins and powerful tails equip them for a life spent bulldozing around in the bottom mud and weeds, in search of food. When moving around the lake, the carp seem to follow particular paths, which anglers come to recognize. Some of these preferred routes have existed for years and it is strange to think that the carp may be patrolling paths that have been used by other fish over centuries.

It might surprise the non-fisher, but carp like these exist as a real community. They really seem to *know* each other and the water they inhabit. Day after day, they will swim around in the same small groups: almost as if they are capable of forming particular friendships. Within each group there is a definite pecking order, with a leader who seems to decide the pattern for the day. These leaders are often older fish, that may well be approaching their sixtieth or even seventieth year. Some are vast, well over three feet long and weighing over thirty pounds.

Even the oldest and largest carp in this lake still look in fabulous condition. None of them have split fins or torn mouths that often results from being caught by anglers, however expert or considerate. Disease is pretty well unknown, since alien fish are never introduced. Death comes gradually to these big fish and when it does, the individual will usually swim off alone, sinking into a torpor for a few days before slowly turning over onto its side.

In front of Chris now, however, there is only rude, healthy appetite. He knows that to trick these fish, he will have to use a completely natural bait in order not to arouse suspicion. His bait box contains lobworms, brandlings and a few big black slugs. He does, however, sprinkle the swim with a few grains of sweet corn. This is one artificial bait that doesn't seem to jar and, from long experience, Chris knows that carp love the sweet yellow grains. The trick works and the scent of the corn draws a couple of fish in close to where Chris wants them.

The carp move slowly over the lake bed, grazing like cows. The fish are really excavating the silt, creating quite noticeable hollows around them as they suck in huge mouthfuls of mud and expel it through their gill flaps, sifting it for food. Bubbles of gas billow from the gills as well and break in a froth on the surface: a sight that experienced carp anglers know well. Carp expel gas from their vents too and these expulsions explain the larger bubbles that burst occasionally a foot or two behind the other eruptions on the surface.

Chris watches the bubble formations hawk-eyed, for they tell him exactly the orientation of the fish in the water and the direction in which it is moving. It shows him precisely where to cast to put the bait right in front of the fish. One cast may be all the chance he gets, before the fish are spooked by his efforts.

Chris still uses a float, rather than the typical leger weight so common these days. He does so not out of any sentiment, but because the float allows him to know exactly where his bait is. This is critical when trying to put a lobworm right on the carp's nose. Provided he has prepared the attack carefully, his first delivery may result in the bait being taken immediately. A dipping float is probably the most sensitive bite indicator of all, since it is so close to the hook. In fact, it will probably begin to tremble and shake slightly as the carp approaches. Once the bait has actually been sucked into the fish's mouth, the float will dip very slowly before moving decisively in one direction or other. This tells Chris not only *when*, but also *how* to strike.

As the hook is set, the water explodes and all hell breaks loose! All thoughts of agues in the joints, of cold, thirst and hunger evaporate in a rush of adrenalin. In that supreme moment, as the rod bucks and the reel whines, Chris is the happiest man in the world.

LEFT: *This beautiful streamlined mirror carp is browsing its way along the sand and gravel bottom, shouldering past fallen masonry. It is absorbed in the process of feeding, its eye constantly swivelling around the socket, looking downwards for any bait or natural foodstuffs present. Its body is inclined at an angle so that the head can dip instantly and suck up any items that look or smell interesting.*

Winter at Warmwell in Dorset on a one-acre carp pool, situated in the middle of a large leisure complex. Chalets stand all around and a dry ski-slope looms above. Fourteen anglers are at the waterside. They include Martin Locke, a tackle and bait manufacturer and a renowned catcher of carp. Martin is here because of one fish, possibly the largest common carp in England. The fish has been named 'Herman' and his weight hovers around fifty pounds. The weather is overcast but mild and there have been reports that fish are on the move.

Carp fishing is so popular today that demand exceeds supply. Today's carp fishers have to pit themselves not only against the fish, but find themselves struggling against each other as well. Many carp waters are lined with anglers almost every day of the year, now that the old statutory close seasons have been abandoned. Over the last decades, a kind of piscatorial arms race has taken place on very many of our carp waters and it has led to a situation that would baffle our angling forebears.

One can analyze what has happened. The more often carp are caught from a particular water, the more wary the fish become and the wiser they get to the methods and tactics employed. To counter this and to keep on catching fish, anglers have continually to devise increasingly sophisticated rigs and new baits. They have to stay a step ahead both of their quarry and their fellow anglers.

The innate wariness of carp, their ability to learn quickly and their longevity, all combine to present the carp angler with enormous challenges. No sooner does a new bait become popular, or a new rig widely adopted, than the fish become wary of them. To stay ahead, a successful carp angler has to keep secret his bait ingredients and guard his tackle modifications from other anglers. Otherwise, they quickly become less effective. And Herman is an extraordinary product of this carp fishing 'arms race'.

The more one thinks about it, the more one appreciates that Herman is a living marvel, a veritable Einstein amongst carp. The statistics are impressive. Consider that there are usually around twenty anglers fishing Herman's pond at any time, in every 24 hours, the whole year round. If we assume that each angler is fishing two rods, then at any given time of day or night all year, there will be forty baits lying around in an area of little more than an acre. Lines are everywhere, criss-crossing the entire pool and encroaching on practically its every square metre.

Herman is a huge fish and he must spend his entire life lifting himself over lines or squeezing underneath them. He must come across baited hooks constantly and there cannot be a single hour of his life when the presence of man does not impinge on his existence.

There cannot be much natural food left in Herman's pond because there are so many other carp, not to mention the ducks, constantly sifting through the silt. This means that Herman is almost totally dependent on anglers' baits to maintain his vast weight. Each time he comes across a group of free offerings, there is likely to be one with a hook in it and every time he eats, the danger is always present of a hook being set and him feeling that familiar persistence drawing him towards the bank. Some of the country's very best anglers are long-term residents at Warmwell and their tackle, rigs and bait are just about as good as they get. Their dedication verges on the fanatical and their concentration unwavering. And yet, despite this mind-bending pressure, Herman succeeds in being caught only a couple or so times a year. Round the clock, for three hundred or so days a year, Herman makes just one or two mistakes: picks up just one or two false baits amongst the tens of thousands that he comes across. Herman is a truly remarkable fish. How on earth does he evade capture for such long periods?

A carp's sight is surprisingly sharp, certainly in clear water. At a couple of metres or so, anything in the water stands out clearly. When a carp moves really close to a bait, details becomes pin sharp. There is a moment just before the fish engulfs the bait when its nose obscures the object, but before that it is subject to the closest scrutiny. Herman also has a good wide angle view of the world and gets a pretty useful impression of anything happening on the bank within a hundred metres or so. Shapes are blurred, but an angler arriving on an exposed bank, for example, will certainly alert a carp more than a football pitch away. Herman is probably constantly aware of people coming and going around his pond and almost certainly sees lines, leads, hook-lengths and probably even the best camouflaged swivels.

Carp have a great sense of smell, though possibly not to rival that of salmon or eels. Herman will be no exception. Carp need these abilities in the wild to detect bloodworms and swan mussels hidden under inches of silt. In a water like Warmwell, Herman will almost certainly be able to detect any abnormal odour on a bait. Many older

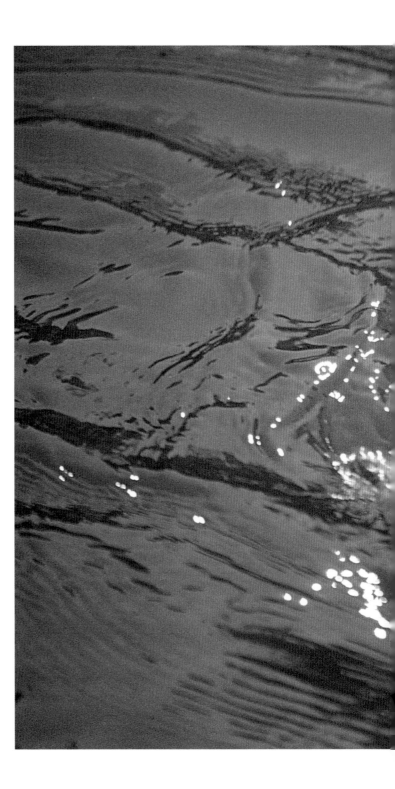

RIGHT: Carp are remarkable fish; they seem almost as happy out of the water as in it. Certainly their diet proves that they are just as happy feeding on the surface of the water as they are on the lake bed. This carp eagerly investigates anything edible it can find on the water's surface – trapped insects, hatching midges or foodstuffs dropped by passing birds. When feeding, carp demonstrate a gusto and an imagination unparalleled by any other fish species.

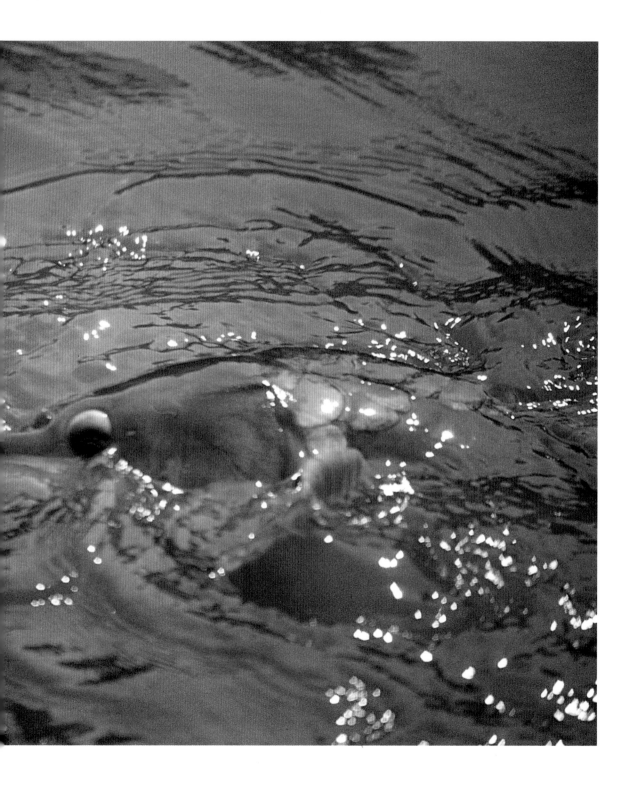

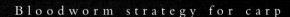
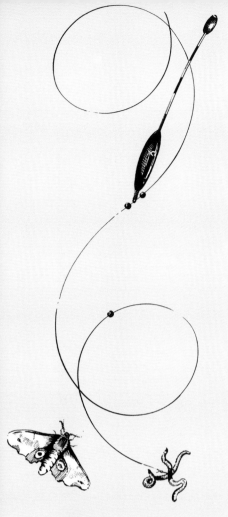

balls of quite firm groundbait such as brown crumb. These balls, about the size of a tangerine, take the bloodworm down to the bottom when introduced into the swim. Once in the water they explode to release dense strongly scented clouds of gyrating bloodworms. As bloodworm are the carps' natural food any passing fish that see or smell the bait will home in and begin feeding.

SWIM

Choose a spot close to a bank where carp regularly patrol and feed. Try fishing under trees or along a drop-off from shallow to deep water. You need to be directly above the bloodworm action so that you can introduce the bait accurately, place your hook bait in precisely the right position and see clearly what is happening. Fishing close in like this is also one of the most exciting forms of sport imaginable.

HOOK BAIT

Bloodworm are tricky to use as hook bait, so try small brandlings or tiny red worms from a compost heap. Two or three red maggots might also serve the purpose. Any small, red, wriggling meaty bait should work well with this method.

PRESENTATION

I prefer a Windbeater float for this method of carp fishing because it is stable and one does not want the bait to move even in a brisk breeze. Shot the float well down so that only the tip is showing. Bites over bloodworm beds are often very delicate because the carp does not charge off with the bait – instead he lies on the bottom, pectoral fins working to maintain position, whilst he hoovers the bait in. Using a couple of

hair-rigged 2-cm-long red worms on a size 8 hook would be an excellent start.

OTHER NATURAL BAITS TO CONSIDER

Carp spend a lot of time feeding on snails and, because of this, one of the most popular and successful baits used in the 1970s was the swan mussel. As a consequence swan mussels were overused during this time. Today, mussels should be used more sparingly, though – it is acceptable to use one as a single bait on occasion. The single swan mussel should be used whole on a large hook such as a size 2. Cast the mussel as close to the carp as possible without scaring it. Do not strike too quickly when the mussel is taken, as the hook does not come away from the bait quickly or cleanly.

Often, late in the evening, when the weather is warm the carp will come to browse on the water surface. This is particularly common in bays into which the wind has been blowing. Here the fish are looking for a carpet of dead insects that have been blown along the water's surface and have piled up in the scum that accumulates against weedbeds and lilypads. Carp give themselves away in this situation by their very gentle movements, and sometimes you can see their backs or heads breaking the surface film. At times like these a large dead moth will be taken with complete confidence. Most carp have eaten hundreds of moths in their lives without being hooked as a result. Of course, finding the moth, hooking it and casting it all come with their own problems. Essentially this is a close-in, creepy-crawly technique.

B loodworm, the tiny red larvae of the common gnat, exist in great carpets in the silt and mud of most lakes and canals. They can be collected from such areas by the experienced angler or bought from the bigger tackle shops, especially those catering for matchmen. However, boodworms are expensive and they are only really needed for very large and wary fish. Other small particle baits like hemp and casters should be tried first and are used in a similar sort of fashion to bloodworm.

INTRODUCING THE BAIT

Bloodworm need to be introduced with care and thought. Keep them in a cool place, or store in the fridge, and before using, dry them between layers of newspaper. When dry, press them into angling books warned against contaminating one's bait with the smell of smoke and tobacco. It is sound advice, for with fish as developed as Herman, every care must be taken to keep hook baits smelling as natural as possible, untainted by suspicious odours.

All carp have a highly discriminating sense of taste, a faculty closely linked to smell. Carp can become really hooked on particular tastes and, for a while, their natural caution may be subjugated. However, they can also remember unpleasant associations and this may be why baits fall from favour after a period of great success.

A carp depends a great deal on its powers of hearing and every time a bait or a lead hits the water, Herman will register it. I have seen carp shy away from bait dropped forty or fifty metres away from them. Even a gun fired half-a-mile off can cause carp to sink out of sight and hide amongst lilypads for an hour or more.

Herman's tactile senses are also highly developed. He will be able to feel lines dragging along his belly or rubbing against his fins and while these sensations no longer cause him to panic, he will gently ease himself away from the danger. His mouth is also extremely touch sensitive and must often detect things that are wrong. He will have learned to mouth baits very gently, testing their feel before swallowing or ejecting them. He can do this so subtly that the angler may feel no sign of it.

Finally, Herman seems to have some kind of sixth sense. It is hard to describe it otherwise and it is something that is possessed by other large carp as well. Without anything apparently being registered by any of his other senses, Herman seems just to *know* when something isn't right. He'll just melt from the scene without the angler or perhaps even the fish knowing why.

Martin Locke has chosen the winter for this latest assault on Herman. He knows that in winter the food levels in the lake will be at their lowest and it is just possible that Herman might be hungry enough to make a mistake. His visit coincides with a long settled spell of mild but overcast weather. It hasn't been cold and there have been some occasional light showers. The wind has also been very light. Carp really detest a fluctuating barometer and unsettled weather. Conditions are now ideal for a pond like this and Martin has decided to make his move.

Martin's approach is rather unusual. Even though his livelihood is as a bait manufacturer, he is avoiding the use of modern boiled baits and rigs

LEFT: Spawning carp explode through shallow, weeded water like a volcanic eruption. In fact, it is not unusual to find a female carp actually lifted right out of the water and pushed onto the bank itself! They concentrate so hard on the shedding of eggs and milt that they are oblivious to any danger or hazard. Spawning generally takes place when the temperature reaches between 17°C and 20°C. The eggs weigh as much as a third of the body weight of a ripe female carp; up to 6000 eggs are produced per pound of body weight.

ABOVE: A view of an entirely different type of lake – Warmwell – a man-made fishery in the south of England. Look at the gravel path surrounding the water and the chalets that dot the banks. The water is cloudy due to the activity of the ducks and the huge head of carp which are continually foraging and competing for food. This does not necessarily make for easy carp fishing: the carp here are as wise as any you will find in Britain and rarely make unforced errors.

altogether. Instead, he is going to use a natural bait to try and hoodwink Herman. On this particular occasion he has chosen bloodworm as an attractor. He has hundreds of thousands of them, wrapped in newspaper and stored in the fridge of one of the chalets. Martin will mix the bloodworms with a fine particle groundbait and some light soil and introduce them into the swim in tennis ball-sized lumps. He is hoping that the imprinted memory of a natural food will stimulate Herman into feeding so enthusiastically that he just might make a mistake. Herman adores bloodworm and to come across so many, especially in winter, is going to be a temptation he will find difficult to resist.

Martin will take even more care over the hook bait. His choice will be either a bunch of bloodworms painstakingly threaded onto a hair, or possibly a bundle of small red worms. These are just a little bit bigger and so possibly a little more attractive, but they will still blend in with the general pattern of groundbaiting. Martin is going to use a light float to avoid the usual splash of a heavy lead. In every way, Martin is trying to make his approach untypical: hoping to come up with a combination that Herman has not seen before and will not register as dangerous.

The night is uneventful, though there is a fair bit of socializing amongst the anglers. Everyone talks of Herman. Where is he at this precise moment? When will he come out again? What bait caught him last time? Will he be over fifty pounds the next time round? When Martin goes off to sleep for a few hours, Herman swims through his dreams: this huge, golden fish hiding so successfully in practically a puddle of water.

The sky starts to lighten shortly after 06.00 and Martin is up and moving cautiously around the lake, past 'bivvies' where other anglers are gently snoring. He heads towards the back of the island. The lake narrows considerably here: just ten or so metres across and heavily wooded on both banks. The water is comparatively shallow also, only a metre or so at the most, with fallen branches providing a real haven of security for any fish. Hardly any anglers fish this bit, as the water is just too rubbish-laden for their methods which depend on long casting and clear swims. Martin is hoping that Herman might decide to have his breakfast here in a little peace and quiet.

The light grows and the drab colours of a dull day emerge. The water is still as mercury and there isn't a sign of a fish. Martin settles back into the undergrowth and scans the channel, up and down. He is quite content to wait hours if necessary. A little after 08.00, the water a few metres to his right begins to ripple ever so slightly. Anyone but a carp expert would probably have overlooked it, but Martin realizes instantly that a big fish has entered the channel: its sheer bulk displacing the water in front of it as it swims along. A tiny cluster of bubbles rises to the surface close to the overhanging branches of a tree. This is it. A fish is closing in and Martin begins to scatter the lightly mixed bloodworm in a carpet right across the channel. The carp will have to cross this band of dancing, gyrating bloodworm and is bound to smell the bait. Once the fish is feeding hard, Martin will make his move.

Soon, heavy swirls rock the surface five metres from Martin's feet. The water is becoming increasingly discoloured as the fish stirs up the bottom, rooting around excitedly for the bloodworm. Could this be Herman? Certainly a lot of water is being displaced so this is a big fish. Then, at last, the sight that Martin wants to see: a large tail fin gently breaks the water's surface for a second, then slides back into the murky brown water. At the root of that tail, the continuous criss-cross pattern of brassy scales that show it is a huge common carp. Martin casts, holding his breath. The red-tipped float settles to within a centimetre of the water surface and he can imagine the four red worms on the hook wriggling on the bottom.

The float shifts and stirs and the water around it rocks as Herman's huge bulk passes nearby. Once, the float jabs down sharply but rises immediately, the line probably caught momentarily round one of herman's fins. A disaster. Herman has dislodged the line without any difficulty, but the seeds of suspicion have been sown. Delightful as the bloodworm taste to him, Herman has discovered that there is no such thing as a free breakfast. Gradually, he drifts away down the channel back into the main pool again. Disconsolate, Martin watches the signs of his departure: a stirring branch; a couple of bubbles and a few dead leaves rising to the surface mark the route. Within five minutes of the float dipping, Herman is once more picking his way over the lines of the slumbering anglers.

Chapter 4

Salmon
Spirit of Silver

IT WAS AUTUMN, WITH SLEET IN THE WIND AND THE ROAR OF rutting stags echoing down from the hill. The river up to the fish traps was brown and foaming and full of roaming salmon. That morning, almost a hundred fish had been caught there and transported by fishery workers to great tanks close by. These fish would later have their eggs and milt stripped at the hatchery, so that their progeny could be used to re-stock the river. Artificially, there would be far fewer fatalities than the wild would allow. Now, though, it was late evening and the fish were at the end of their great round journey, milling around in frustration under the spout, provided to supply them with freshly oxygenated water. One great cock fish, red and hook-jawed, tried repeatedly to leap up the column of water: thrashing against it with his tail and trying to force his weary head into the pipe itself, as if searching for his true spawning grounds. The fish probably hadn't eaten for months and was living off its last reserves of stored fat. Even now, blind purpose drove him on. So close to death, the spirit of life still burned within him.

The life of the salmon is a heroic one. The saga begins when the eggs are laid during the winter months in the gravel beds of well-oxygenated and fast-flowing streams. At between three and four months, the egg hatches out into an alevin: a minute translucent creature with an

LEFT: Salmon predators prey on the fish throughout its lifecycle – from parr to maturity, from the redds to the feeding grounds in the Atlantic Ocean. The otter is no exception. Otters consume vast amounts of parr and smolts as well as mature fish returning to the redds to spawn. Even kelts, salmon that have spawned and are dropping back to the sea, are not safe. Otters also do a great deal of good too, especially by combing up vast numbers of eels which would otherwise prey on salmon eggs and growing parr. Intriguingly, studies on otters along the River Dee catchment area reveal that most salmon caught and killed by them are males, mainly because males spend more time on the breeding grounds than females. As a dominant male salmon can fertilize the eggs of several females, the salmon population can better withstand the loss of males than of females. Otters, of course, do not know this but here is more proof that nature works in fascinating and mysterious ways.

 umbilical sac attached to its throat. For four or five weeks the baby salmon lives off its shrinking yolk sac, after which it forces its way out of its natal gravel and emerges as a tiny salmon fry. It now has to fend for itself and seek its food, embarking on a life beset with many dangers.

Nature is not entirely unhelpful, though. At this early stage, the little fish is covered in spots and acquires a shadowy pattern of vertical bars along its flanks. This makes an effective camouflage against the gravel of the river bottom. The baby salmon is now known as a parr and, to the untutored eye, looks identical to a brown trout at a similar stage of development. Salmon parr feed on insects and other invertebrates such as shrimps and snails. But the parr themselves are hunted by a host of enemies. Pike; perch; chub; eels; large trout; otters; mink; herons; kingfishers; mergansers; cormorants; goosanders and grebes all feast on parr and decimate the original number of hatchling fish.

At about two years of age, the salmon parr starts to undergo extraordinary physiological changes that prepare it for a new environment. The fish's scales gradually change to a bright silver colour. Now, at about 15 cm, the fish is known as a smolt and in late spring migrates downriver and out to the sea. Once again, the immature salmon runs a gauntlet of enemies: gulls; cormorants again; shags; bass; pollack; conger eels and cod. Just about everything it seems has a greedy eye open for the passing shoals of silver smolt. Those that survive head out to sea, where they feed on the ocean's bounty. Once at sea, the salmons' growth rate accelerates. At the end of the first year at sea, they will be twenty to thirty times heavier than when they quit the river. Thereafter, the growth rate lessens only gradually. Some salmon, like those of the small rivers of Devon, return to their native rivers after just a year at sea and are known as 'grilse'. Others come back after two or more years at sea and these fish are called 'maiden' salmon. A comparatively few fish will stay out at sea for four summers and these return as real monsters, some over forty pounds in weight.

Quite how the salmon manages to locate the river of its birth and return to the spawning gravels whence it originated from the egg is a fascinating story and only partly understood. Recent research suggests that salmon are equipped to navigate using the earth's magnetic field. However, once in coastal waters, it is almost certainly the salmon's fantastic sense of smell that enables it finally to locate its own particular river.

The salmon has become almost symbolic of the purest water and a totem of man's nostalgia for undefiled nature. We like to hark back to a time when the London's river Thames teemed with running salmon. The recent return of salmon to the Thames after long absence has taken on a particular significance in the causes of 'environment' and 'conservation'.

The relationship between salmon and the water is of central importance to the angler. The behaviour of the fish is largely determined by the height of the river and its temperature and whether these are rising or falling. These factors, in turn, influence the angler's choice of method and, indeed, the prospects for catching a fish. Salmon fishers will argue till Domesday on the subjects of air and water temperatures; the ideal height of the river and on the interminable subject of size and colour of lure. While some consensus is achieved on general matters, the fine details fuel endless discussions in the bars of fishing hotels. Perhaps the greatest enigma is that salmon take the angler's lure *at all*. By the time they return to the river, salmon have long since given up feeding and live off reserves of fat stored in their tissues.

On October 7th 1922, a certain Miss Georgina Ballantine was fishing with her father on Perthshire's River Tay above Caputh Bridge, near Murthly. It was to be an historic day.

Miss Ballantine was born, lived and died in a cottage just a good cast away from the Boat Pool. It was on this pool that she hooked and did battle with a huge salmon that turned out to be the British record. Her father was the registrar of the area and friend of Sir Alexander Lyle, of Glendelvine estate, and he and his daughter were standing in for the laird who was unable to fish that day.

It was Saturday and late in the afternoon when Miss Ballantine began to fish with a small natural bait: a two-inch dace that her father had put onto a Malloch's spinning mount. Darkness was starting to fall and her father had just looked at his watch and remarked that it was nearly time to leave when the salmon took hold. It was 6.15 p.m. For a while, the fish moved slowly downriver, tempting Mr Ballantine to land the boat to try and play the fish from the bank. Once ashore, however, Miss Ballantine knew she had a fight on her hands. Surging off

ABOVE: A pair of migrating salmon swim upstream through a fish pass. The smaller fish is probably a female whereas the big fish in the background might well be a dominant male, a fish capable of chasing parr and competing males off the spawning sites.

LEFT: Salmon can cover distances of up to twenty miles a day when they are pushing upstream to the spawning redds. Most fish run at night or as the sun begins to set or rise. The fish are particularly vulnerable when running through shallow water and stickles, when their backs are frequently exposed and can be seen by predators. November and December are the common spawning months in most rivers; the feverish activity takes place along the gravel runs where the redds can easily be cut.

Over the last seventy years, tackle and techniques have improved greatly but a great deal of what Wood proposed still holds good. Lines no longer have to be greased, of course, but the concept of the small, slimline fly fished very close to the surface is still adhered to when air and water temperatures begin to rise. There are several considerations to bear in mind when using this method: the line is probably best double-tapered and coloured white to make a delicate presentation and to indicate precisely what is happening out of the water. The leader ought also to be matched with the fly, the size of the fish and the power of the water. A small fly on a heavy leader does not fish well and points of between eight and ten pounds breaking strain are about right. It is vital that the fly does not skate across the river but actually sinks up to fifteen centimetres below the surface. A multi-hooked fly is more difficult to sink than a single-hooked fly because of its extra bulk which causes more drag in the water.

B ack in the 1920s A.H.E. Wood turned the salmon world upside down with his discoveries on the River Dee. Briefly, his theories were that the fly should fish close to the surface when the air is warmer than the water; the fly should cross the fish slowly and at a broadside angle; the line should float, be mended and be thoroughly controlled as the fly is fished and that the hooking procedure should be left to the power of the current as much as possible. Wood also simplified both the number and the dressing of the fly patterns until he was quite happy to fish with just three types of differing sizes, each sparsely dressed. He tried to watch the fish and the take and likened the game to super nymphing with lighter rods, line and a far greater delicacy than known before in the salmon world.

Equally, a sparsely dressed single hook may sink faster and truer than one that is overelaborate. Moving to a slightly larger hook, for example from an 8 to a 6, might also give a bit of extra weight. It's also worthwhile sinking the leader if necessary and there are several brands of material on the market that will achieve this.

The fly must be fished intelligently: if the water is very still then a cast across river can be made and the fly can be worked back by hand. If, however, there is a brisk current then it's important to cast well downstream and let the fly hang over the most likely water. It's also a good idea to hold the rod at right angles so that the slowest possible fly speed across the current is achieved. Lastly, it is often vital in a fast current to 'mend' the line once the cast has been made in order to try to prevent a large loop being formed which will pull the fly quickly off course.

Do remember that in low, clear conditions, salmon can be easily spooked and are just as wily as trout. In all types of salmon fishing, but particularly when using the floating line, approach the water cautiously and avoid making any vibration or shadow as you move.

downstream, the salmon passed under Caputh Bridge: the line cutting Georgina's fingers as she gamely tried to slow things down. Fortunately, the salmon went through the near, north side arch of the bridge and she was able to stumble after him along the bank. It was nearly dark now and the salmon continued downstream, slower perhaps, but still with such inexorable power that Mr Ballantine returned for the boat so that they could follow the fish. His daughter was now clearly feeling the strain and was calling the fish the 'Beast'.

At this stage in the fight, without the boat, the fish would have been lost. It took off irresistibly to the other side of the river, towards an island a quarter-of-a-mile downstream. All the Ballantines could do was to follow the fish across the darkening Tay. They landed again on the island above the Burbane Pool. Though there was no light to see the salmon, they could tell that it was close from the angle of the line to the water. Mr Ballantine felt along the line until he came to the swivel. Knowing the length of the trace, he estimated the position of the fish and decided to risk gaffing the salmon unseen. His judgement was unerring and the point found its mark. The time was 8.20 p.m. and the two-hour fight had taken them half-a-mile down the river. Before them lay a truly monstrous salmon. It weighed 64 pounds, was four feet six inches long and had a girth of $28^1/2$ inches. The fish was only slightly pink along its flanks and still had some sea lice clinging: a giant fresh run autumn salmon, straight from the sea.

To land such a fish in the dark and on the comparatively unreliable tackle of the day was a colossal feat. Miss Ballantine has deservedly held this most prestigious of records for three-quarters of a century and earned herself an immortal place in angling history.

The fish itself is well worth examining. Firstly, it had grown massive by spending three winters and four summers at sea, where it would have fed heavily on small fish and crustaceans. From leaving the Tay as a tiny smolt in early 1919, the fish had piled on weight in preparation for its return to the spawning redds, in the final autumn of its life. Why the fish had stayed so long at sea and gained such vast size provides fascinating speculation. Sex comes into it, for Miss Ballantine's salmon was male as virtually all massive salmon prove to be. It is a fact that both the smallest and the very largest sexually mature salmon happen to be male fish.

The life's purpose of any male salmon is to procreate: to fertilize the

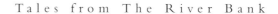

RIGHT: The River Tay in summer when water levels are low and the river bed is exposed. There are few fish in the river at such times. Those fish that are present tend to hug the deeper pools, waiting for rain to swell the shallows and allow them to forge on upstream. Tay salmon can grow very large indeed and therefore need the extra security of deeper water.

 eggs shed by a female fish on the gravel bed of the headwater of some river. There are essentially three contrasting strategies for achieving this. The first possibility is for a male fish to become a sexually precocious parr! In some cases, salmon can actually become sexually mature and join the mating activity when only a tiny parr. One advantage of this might be that a parr is too small to be noticed easily by the adult males, who would otherwise chase it away as competition. It can shed its milt and be away probably without the adults – male or female – being aware of its presence. Another advantage in the precocious parr strategy is that the small fish have a chance of surviving the conjugal act, unlike the majority of the fully adult male salmon. The fish can then develop normally as a smolt, go to sea and subsequently return as an adult for a second crack of the procreative whip. However, the strategy is not without risk. Most obviously, small parr can easily be killed by big adult males. Further, sexual maturation represses the natural immune system, leaving the parr more susceptible to disease.

Some male salmon return after just one year at sea, as small but sexually mature grilse. A high proportion of returning grilse in many rivers is male. The problem facing these male grilse is that they can be bullied off the redds by larger, fully grown salmon, so this strategy is not the perfect solution to the mating game either.

Miss Ballantine's fish opted for the third strategy. It grew very large by staying at sea for four years and feeding. Such huge salmon are comparatively rare, but when they do return to the river, they are powerful enough to dominate the spawning redds, take the pick of the hen fish and chase away any competition. But even this strategy is not perfect. To gain pole position back in the river, the salmon has to spend longer out in the hazardous ocean. The larger it becomes, the bigger and more noticeable a target it presents to the many salmon predators. Sharks, bears, seals and killer whales are just some of the creatures that prey on salmon and against which even a sixty-pound fish has little defence.

It has been calculated that a salmon's maximum speed can be up to ten times its body length, per second. Thus, the larger the fish, the faster it can swim. Miss Ballantine's Beast would therefore have had speed as well as size in its favour: in theory travelling up to 20 m.p.h. One wonders how many times during the Beast's battle with Miss Ballantine its speed and weight might nearly have won him his freedom: certainly that initial current assisted surge downriver towards the bridge must have been virtually impossible to contain.

And just why did that fish snap at Miss Ballantine's dace in the dusk of an October afternoon? Did the fish act out of anger, irritation, frustration, or simple boredom? In all probability, a salmon takes the angler's bait purely as a feeding reflex. In fresh water, the fish has no need to feed. This has to be, since no salmon river could provide enough food to sustain a run of adult salmon if they needed to draw nourishment from the stream. By the time the salmon reaches coastal waters, hunger has been switched off by its internal chemistry. But for so long during its ocean feeding the fish has reacted instinctively to the flash of small fish. One more, dangled right in front of its nose, elicits an automatic if not volitional response.

A further interesting debate concerns the relationship between large salmon and women anglers. It is a matter of record that several notable salmon (large cock fish) have been caught by women. This is particularly noteworthy since 'sisters of the angle' have historically formed a distinct minority. It has been postulated that natural scents given off by female anglers – pheromones – are either attractive or possibly *less repulsive* to the fish than those emitted by male fishermen. The case is far from proven, but certainly the salmon has amazing olfactory powers and displays demonstrable reaction to the faintest of chemical stimuli.

In the case of Miss Ballantine's salmon, the pheromone theory probably falls down, since it was her father who handled the bait and mounted it on the tackle. If anything, it would have been his odours that were present. It is probably much fairer to Miss Ballantine if we remember her as a skilful and doughty angler, who just happened to be in the right place, at the right time!

Mid August on the River Dee, outside the Banchory Lodge Hotel. The river is low, warm and clear.

Roddy, the gillie, walked down the hotel's lawns, looked out at the river before him and knew that catching salmon on such a day would be very difficult indeed. Nevertheless, there were plenty of fish in the pool and this always presented a chance, however slim. The salmon had been there for days, if not weeks, prevented by the low water from trekking further

RIGHT: Dusk and dawn are the prime times for salmon fishing. At such times the salmon begin to show an interest in their surroundings and consider pushing on upstream. This angler has positioned himself in the shallow run to a deep pool in the hope that some salmon are beginning to leave the security of the snags and boulders to forge on upstream, close to his carefully positioned bait.

LEFT: This is one of the most magnificent and rarest members of the salmon family – the taimen of far eastern Asia. Very few of these magnificent creatures have been caught or even seen. Their lifestyles are similar to the Atlantic salmon, apart from the fact that they do not leave their rivers and go to sea. Rather, they live for very long periods of time, spawning again and again and growing larger and larger in the process. In particular, their heads become very heavy and well developed through years of predatorial life. There are unconfirmed reports of these extraordinary land-locked salmon reaching 125 pounds or even 150 pounds in weight.

No matter how early or late in the season or how cold the water is, a salmon will take a fly if it can be seen and if it is presented perfectly. Salmon are not easy fish to tempt though: they live in a near torpor, unwilling to leave their secure lies and certainly not willing to chase a fly moving quickly over their heads. It is vital, therefore, to get a visible fly right down among the fish and to move it slowly and methodically, as close to their noses as possible. A boat can be very useful in these circumstances as it puts the fisherman in the best position to present a fly with absolute precision in a known taking area.

Generally, a medium-sink, double-taper fly line is the perfect starter for cold conditions, although a fast line can play its part in very deep, dark pools when the fish are stubbornly remaining on the bottom. It is tempting to go for big rods and heavy lines under these conditions but the angler must not over-rod himself and thus lose control of his tackle, especially when there is a strong wind about. A fourteen or fifteen-foot rod is about right even for a large river but it's sensible to go shorter if the pools allow it.

Fly choice is all important in cold water early in the season and it is vital that whatever is used makes a strong impression on the salmon. If the fish are lying half-frozen in deep water their reactions will be much slower than those of summer fish, and they will not be willing to come to the surface to chase flies across a pool. A six to eight-centimetre tube is the correct size for a medium to large river, a fly with bright attention-grabbing colours like hot orange, red, yellow and black. When sleet and snow-melt fill a river a large conspicuous-looking fly should be used.

It is essential to visualize what the fly's movements are in the pool, to work it, to instil life into it and yet to make sure that it is searching every possible salmon-holding lie as thoroughly as possible. In icy conditions when the water is lifeless, the fly has to practically tap a salmon on the nose before a take is induced. Even then, and after a slow, gentle draw on the line as the fish rises slightly from the bottom, the salmon may well sink back down to sanctuary behind a boulder once again.

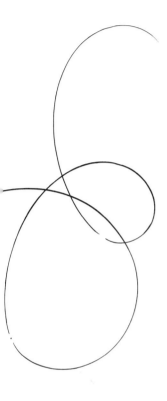

upriver towards their spawning grounds. Stale summer salmon like this are notoriously hard to tempt. They find the low, warm, poorly oxygenated water enervating. Quite apart from the lethargy of the fish, these conditions present purely mechanical difficulties for the angler as well. Without a decent flow to work the fly, it looks hideously artificial: an inert confection of fur and feather, rather than a creature of life and vitality.

After rain, the river is cooler and better oxygenated. Not only are the fish livelier and more receptive, but the faster swirling current helps hide imperfections in the angler's lure or presentation.

To make Roddy's job even more difficult, the hotel guests had been flogging the pool over the preceding days and the salmon were well aware of it. These were now very nervy salmon and easily scared from their lies. On top of this, an otter had been visiting the pool just before dawn for several days, making the fish even more skittish.

It is immediately obvious why the big pool in front of the hotel is favoured by so many fish. There is a deep channel running along the north bank which provides some protection from the sun and the attentions of fishermen and even herons. A smaller stream, the Feugh, also enters from this bank and provides a flush of cooler water and an increased choice of currents and lies. At the head of the pool large stones break up the current and create a heavy riffle. In low summer conditions, this broken water helps add a bit of oxygen into the stale Dee.

It is not particularly hard to catch salmon in perfect conditions when the river is at a good level and fish are teeming through. It is much harder when the water is low, clear and warm. Under such conditions an angler really has to fish skilfully to stand any chance. Roddy's approach was as cautious as possible, for he knew that the pool had suffered more than its fair share of angling pressure over the past few days. Despite entering the water as carefully as possible, one fish was roused and flopped listlessly out of the water.

Roddy was using a floating line and a tiny black fly. Starting at the top, he worked his way down the pool, methodically and with total control: casting twice from each stance, then dropping two paces down-river before casting again. The fly was put across the river and slightly downstream, then worked across in a steady movement. Each time, as the fly swung round some 15–20 cm below the surface, Roddy's

LEFT: A salmon caught and displayed for a second by flashlight. The surrounding foliage tells us that autumn has arrived and, therefore, this fish is not far from its spawning beds. There is only one thing to do at this time of the year and that is to release the salmon gently back into the water so that it can continue its journey for the last two or three months of its life and fulfil nature's purpose for it.

concentration was total. He knew that if a take came it might be the merest of tweaks.

This was exactly what happened. The salmon took halfway down the pool registering as a gentle tightening of the line and nothing more. Roddy did not strike, but merely lifted into the fish. There was an immediate boil on the surface; then the salmon dived for the bottom, searching for the security of its lie. The fish shook its head twice, sending vibrations up the line. Then the hook fell out. Roddy was not in the least concerned. He had intended releasing the fish anyway. Instead, his satisfaction lay in having deceived a stale and jaded fish. Things would change for the better when the westerlies swept across Scotland, bringing with them clouds and rain.

The River Barle on Exmoor at Tarr Steps. Early September. After weeks of dry summer, heavy rain had been falling on the moor for many hours. The river was rising fast and colouring.

Chris Rowe was one of the few that year to see the Barle salmon running in any numbers. Both the summer and autumn had been dry and the first week of September witnessed virtually all of that year's run of fish pass under the ancient stone clapper bridge across the river. It was quite a sight. The salmon had been chafing in the estuary for weeks, if not months. With the sudden rise in the river, they were now free to run home and they did so now with an urgency that entranced the watching fisherman as he sat on the masonry of the bridge at dawn.

Barely a minute would pass without a salmon showing, sometimes almost brushing Rowe's feet as it hurdled the cascades of soil-stained water. The river was at last welcoming them home, as the temperatures fell and the oxygen level rose. The coloured spate water seemed to give the fish a sense of security, while the added volume allowed passage, where for weeks previously, the river had been a sorry series of tepid pools linked by thin trickles.

As the light grew slowly, Rowe could make out details of the fish flocking past him. They were small for salmon – around five to eight pounds – but normal for the river, as the little Barle is not suited to larger fish. Many were beginning to colour red and pink: their enforced sojourn in fresh water tarnishing the majestic silver minted in the sea. A few fish, though, were not coloured. These had obviously journeyed many miles overnight and had come up straight from the sea without pause. One salmon in particular caught Rowe's eye. A deep cut down its left flank, running from the dorsal to the ventral fin, revealed a gash of red flesh. Probably caused by an otter or seal, the wound had not impaired the salmon's primal urge and Rowe admired the fish even more for it.

The fisherman walked up the valley. As the low cloud began to lift slightly, a pallid sunshine illuminated the dripping forest, but the river continued to rise. The fish were now beginning to come to rest, taking up daytime lies in the pools, under trees and around rocks. Some even pushed themselves into tight crevices with only their tails showing. In slower deeper pools, like the Hind's Pit a mile or so upriver, there was still activity as fish jumped and searched for lies. Henry Williamson, Rowe's favourite country writer, once suggested that a salmon leaps in order to take in the sights it recognized from its youth, perhaps even looking for the pool it had spent its days in as a parr.

A little before midday, the flood had reached its height and the river was strewn with branches and leaves. Some salmon were still noticeable in the shallow water: recent arrivals, scurrying around looking for shelter. A few fish sought refuge in patches of long grass that had been submerged by the spate, but most took up station behind the larger rocks, betrayed by the occasional glint of a silver flank in the sun. The river had quietened down now. Some small brown trout could be seen rising in the slack water out on the flooded field. Ever opportunists, these diminutive trout had ventured out over erstwhile dry land, looking for terrestrial morsels forced out by the rising water.

Small spate rivers can lose their colour and height quickly after the rain stops and by late afternoon Rowe thought it worthwhile to set up a rod. Fly choice was not a problem: something large and gaudy. It would need to be something the salmon could see easily in water still carrying a heavy stain. Tying on the biggest black and orange affair in his fly box, he dropped it over the Tarr Steps bridge, noticing that it was still visible a foot below the surface.

He took his time working upriver, casting accurately to any likely lie. Once, a dark-coloured fish actually came up to his fly and rolled over it, making a boil on the surface and a pause in his heart beat. By the time

ABOVE: Waterfalls like these present no barrier to the returning salmon whose desire to reach the redds conquers almost all obstacles. The leaping ability of salmon has been exaggerated but the reality is dramatic enough. A perpendicular jump of 12 feet has been reliably recorded. That is a similar feat to a man vaulting over a 30 foot bar with no pole or aid of any sort – and against a howling wind!

LEFT: It is bliss to be out on a Devon stream at dawn like this. The light is subdued, perfect for instilling confidence in the fish. Best of all, a heavy flood the previous day is beginning to fine down and water clarity is almost perfect. The angler also knows that there will be fresh fish in the pool that he is fishing.

he had reached Black Pool, the river had lost more of its colour. Now he could see his fly half-a-metre down. He approached the pool extremely cautiously. The light was going now and the rain had started falling again. Here, if anywhere, was the chance of a fish, provided he didn't disturb the pool. Even with the stream thundering all around them salmon are cautious creatures, alert to things happening around them in the water and above it.

Creeping to the head of the pool, Rowe cast out into the fast water. Almost immediately, the line sang tight. A fish stationed behind one of the stones in the neck of the pool had seen the fly and made an instant decision to take. The fight was dramatic, with the splashes of the leaping fish echoing, amplified, off the sheer rock walls of the pool. An early roosting pigeon was startled by the commotion, its wings clapping as it flew away in the wet evening. As the angler eventually drew the beaten fish to the bank, its flank gleamed in the twilight. Rowe marvelled at how huge even a modest fish can look when caught from such a tiny river. He knelt on the gravel beside it and fumbled for his priest to make the kill. It was then, in the nick of time, that the fish flopped over to reveal its other flank. Instantly, the angler recognized the deep scar. Knowing that he could not finish what otter or seal had started, Rowe quickly slipped the fish back into the Barle and walked back to the Steps with the rain washing his beaming face.

The salmon resumed its lie in the fast water, perhaps shocked by its recent experience, but not one whit deterred from its true purpose. The following weeks saw the fish force its way upriver, past Withypool to Simon's Bath and beyond, seeking out the feeder stream to keep an appointment with destiny.

By November, the fish was in the shallow stream awaiting the arrival of the hen fish. By now, as winter closed in, the females had lost all their silver sea beauty and were dark, almost black, with bulging over-ripe bellies. The scarred male had himself acquired his rust and red mating livery and his head was now disfigured by a huge hooked lower jaw: the 'kype' by which a male salmon can be instantly recognized, even at a distance.

Close to the culmination of his life the male found his mate. As she prepared her nest, the cock fish kept station beside her, alert to any intruder upon this final sacred act. To make the 'redd', the female fish turned on her side and beat her tail vigorously on the stream bed. Her flapping tail disturbed the small stones which drifted away a few inches in the current and left a shallow depression in the gravel. At last, when satisfied that the nest was ready, the hen fish pressed her abdomen hard down into the little hollow she had made. Instinctively, the male fish drew close alongside and just a little forward of her and started to quiver violently. This was the stimulus for the hen fish to shed her eggs. The mouths of both fish gaped wide open as they reached climax. A stream of pale orange spawn extruded from her vent, mixing instantly with the milky cloud of milt that spurted simultaneously from his.

Spent and disoriented, his life's work completed, the male fish drifted off a few metres downstream. His mate, meanwhile, had one final task to complete. Just a little upstream of the nest, the exhausted hen fish repeated the same tail flapping exercise she had used to cut the redd. This time her purpose was to cover the precious fertilized eggs: to bury them under a protective layer of gravel and small stones.

By the end of January, both male and female salmon were dead, but under the gravel of the stream bed their eggs were preparing to hatch. In three or four years these would be adult salmon and they would be surging up under the arches of the clapper bridge on a late summer flood.

Chapter 5

The Eel
Visitor from the Sargasso Sea

WADING THE WYE AT SUNSET, I APPROACHED THE TAIL OF A DEEP pool overhung by a large willow. From the roots of the tree appeared a very large eel, which began to comb the shallows in front of me, searching for supper. There was just enough light from the sky to illuminate the water and give it a shadow-dappled mystery that suited the eel perfectly. It looked magnificent, its skin a bright jade green and its eyes glowing pale yellow. It was an almost indescribable colour, like some rare and precious jewel. The sinuous movement of its body was also mesmeric, effortless and efficient. It caught two gudgeon with ease before starting to uproot stones with its big, powerful head to grub for caddis, snails and leeches. Then the fish and its beauty were lost to me, enveloped in the darkness. The eel could continue its mysterious secret life unobserved beneath the inky surface.

An early June evening on a large Norfolk Broad. The weather is hot and humid and the day has been still with little breeze. The Broad is several hundred acres in extent and fringed with reed beds.

'Row harder, boy', William said to me. His instructions were delivered in a broad Norfolk dialect and involved much swearing as he hung over the stern of the boat laying hundreds of metres of fyke net alongside the beds of Norfolk reed. 'If you don't row faster and get that net tight, the

LEFT: This photograph is interesting because it shows how hard an eel's life is with so many predators to avoid. This eel met its ghastly fate in the beak of a great crested grebe. The eel was caught in the centre of Norwich, in the River Wensum, and resisted its captor for a full 45 minutes during which time the grebe travelled upstream, tussling with it, for almost three-quarters of a mile. The eel resisted by twining its body around the grebe's beak and neck in an effort to gain some purchase and prise itself away from danger. The grebe, however, was equally determined and finally won the battle.

eels won't go in it. They like to feel it hard against their bodies and if it goes in slack we won't have an eel come morning.' I rowed till my eyeballs popped and still the eel-catcher was barely satisfied. He looked pityingly at me, his eyes screwed up tightly against the fireball of the setting sun.

Thankfully, the last net was finished with, laid in water a metre deep. We could now head back across the Broad, row down the dyke and land on the piece of rough ground that served for his garden. His cottage was already half hidden in the shadows of the alder wood. It is hard not to caricature William as some a sort of wrinkled and wizened old eel shaman. There were eels in the smoke-house next door and eels alive in the trap by the boathouse. There was eel slime on the door handle and his clothes were smeared everywhere with the stuff. He wore an eel-skin belt and the smell of eels pervaded everything. He told me the house was actually built on a raft over the oozing marsh, so there were probably eels under the house as well. But William is no caricature. Eels were simply his profession, nothing more, nothing less. He had to know as much about them as possible, for his living depended on it. As a young man, though, he told me that he had wanted to drive a steam engine!

To talk to William about eels is to enter a strange world where sound country lore and observation is mingled with myth and nonsense. His conversation is full of the most unbelievable assertions, but one has to remember that they are based on sixty years' experience. By the end, fact and fantasy seem to mingle, with the eels occupying a place alongside witches and ghosts, will-o-the-wisps and men from Mars!

'Eels are the lost wanderers from Atlantis, you know', he said. 'For hundreds of thousands of years, the eels left our shores and made their way there to spawn. Then they rested in the beautiful lakes and pools before returning. But when the land in the west was lost to the sea, the eels were deprived of their resting place. Now they die in the sea, too tired to make it back to their homeland.'

Scientists will draw a deep breath at such a tale, but it does have some similarity with what is known of the eel's actual life story: its extraordinary migration out to the Sargasso Sea in the western Atlantic, where it breeds and dies. What is quite miraculous, however, is how the minute larval eels make the huge journey back across the Atlantic. The thousands of miles travelled by these elvers is as fascinating to scientists as it is to William. Perhaps they are guided by the sun, moon and the stars; or maybe some exceptional sense of smell. It has been suggested that they may navigate by using the earth's magnetic field. It may simply be that these little fish are such feeble swimmers that they are transported inexorably by ocean currents: the Gulf Stream and North Atlantic Drift.

'What is certain', William went on to say, 'is that the elver run begins in the springtime when water temperatures begin to rise, sometime towards late March or early April. The elvers tend to run for around five nights, generally close to the Full Moon when the tide is high. This is the only time when the downstream flow of the lower rivers is reversed and allows the elvers to make it upriver. The elvers start to run at dusk, the incoming tide pushing them in a great wave up from the sea. As the tide turns, the elvers leave the centre of the river and run along the banks where there is more shelter from the current. They will swim against the river flow for as long as they can, then rest where they can find shelter and wait until the next tide takes them another stage further upriver.' It is during the ebb, when the elvers seek the shelter of the banks, that William can fish for them: holding his nets in the water facing downstream, waiting for the tiny pin-like fish to be washed into the mesh.

Despite the huge number of casualties, millions of elvers survive to reach quiet waters where they live and grow for several years until they reach sexual maturity and are seized by the urge to procreate. The rich shallow Norfolk Broads around William's cottage abound with eels and he has fished for them all his life.

'Eels are not scavengers' he tells me. 'When I lay my long-lines with hundreds of baited hooks I must use fresh fish with the blood flowing and the scales still tight to the body, or freshly dug worms. If the bait isn't fresh I just won't catch anything worth going out for. Everything has to be killed that day and be clean. If you put old fish on, all that you will get is pike that will root-up any rotting fish.' (Pike anglers will probably disagree with William on this one.) 'Eels live on daphnia, tadpoles, frogs and fish: just about anything alive or just dead and they've got such a strong sense of smell they are put off by anything rancid. Watch them attack a whole small roach on one of the long-lines. They'll grasp the tail and writhe around with it, their teeth embedded, trying to pull out a chunk of flesh to go away and chew. But I hook them up so that they can't get away with it. Eventually they'll swallow the lot and get caught.

LEFT: *I would love to say that this is a photograph of an eel taken at dawn as it slithers its way across wet grass towards a new watery home. Unfortunately, it is not. This is an eel which has been caught by an angler, unhooked and allowed to rest for a moment before being returned to the lake.*

You get the better eels if you use big baits. Small baits only get small fish and there's no money in them.

'A big eel is a wily one all right and I know for sure that if I prick one on a long-line and it gets off, then it will leave the water. I know this is true. I've seen them travelling over land many times and that's a fact. Elvers follow dykes and drains and ditches, but yellow eels will cross meadows and go through the marsh on mild nights, specially when there's been rain enough to make the ground wet. And as for silver eels (those that have finished feeding and are about to travel westward to spawn with their vents actually sealed), they will cross anything to get to a stream that will lead them eventually to the sea.' Having spent hundreds of dawns on meadows on just such days myself, without having seen a wandering eel, I still have to doubt what William told me.

'It's when eels are travelling overland that their senses are most alert and I reckon that's why most people don't even see them. The eels hear them or see them coming miles off. You've got to stand as quiet as a heron. If you tramp about then the eels will just disappear and lie low. I even saw one go into a rabbit burrow once! You've got to remember that eels can breathe through their skin for quite a while, so that's not as unlikely as it sounds. If you don't believe me and you don't take the trouble to see them, then you won't. And that's the long and short of it.

'Of course, there's all sorts of other ways that eels can arrive at improbable places you would think would be impossible for them to get to. They used to be stocked as elvers into all sorts of remote little pits and ponds around the place, especially before the War when I was a lad. Me and my uncle used to cycle around everywhere with pails of elvers on our handlebars and I dare say some of those fish are alive today. Then again, eels could be dropped by herons or grebes that have bitten off a bigger mouthful than they can chew. Floods push them about a bit. You've got to remember that the eel has a long life: sixty years or more if they don't choose to go off to the Sargasso Sea earlier. And a lot can happen in nature during that time, especially to an active sort of fish like the eel that likes to investigate everything.

'Of course, eels will sulk for long periods, especially if they've got a full stomach and there's nothing they like better than hiding in old pipes. They can actually swim in backwards if they want and they've got a tail like a monkey's that can pull them up into nooks and crannies where you'd think they could never reach. They hide up more in waters where there are lots of pike and they'll choose their times carefully to go out and about. If there aren't many pike, eels are a free-swimming sort of fish, but it's pike, along with otters, cormorants, herons and grebes that are their biggest enemies. Pike will even dig them up in the winter – actually out in the mud itself.' (Pike anglers discovered fifteen years ago that hardly anything beats a section of eel for a bait.) 'The interesting thing is that pike don't eat the tench and I've often seen groups of tench with their heads buried in the silt and their tails waving around. I've gone up to them and pushed them around with the oar and they don't swim off. You would think they'd be really easy prey but the pike leave them alone. The eels aren't so lucky and many is the pike I've cooked that's been packed with them.

'There's so much that the eel knows and you've got to keep up if you're going to catch them and make a living. For example, the eels in this Broad know exactly when and where the bream and roach will spawn: to the day, to the hour even! That's why we've been laying our nets here tonight and I'll guarantee tomorrow morning we'll have a haul that will make your eyes bulge. There are times when you see the eels run in amongst the spawning roach, actually gobbling the eggs up as they come out of the vent. At other times, especially when there are pike about as there are here, they'll lie low till night, until after the eggs have been laid. Then they'll slide their way in and that's when they'll eat and that's when we'll catch them. There'll be another high point in four or five weeks or so when the tench begin to spawn – always around bulrushes this time, over the hardest bit of lake bed that you can find. Mind you, there are less tench these days and less eggs and there won't be so many eels, but it's still worth keeping an eye open for them. It's in the spring that I do the best, apart from the autumn when the silvers are running out to sea.

'I used to have an eel-trap on the mill-race where the river becomes tidal. My grandfather owned it first, so it dates way back. But there were so many cogs, chains and rusty ironwork, it was the devil to keep up, so twenty years ago I let the whole thing rot. On a good night, though, I could easily net a hundred silvers, with some big ones amongst them.

'Like the elver run, the silvers' migration back to the sea is easily predictable once you know. You want a night of a New Moon, because

ABOVE: A hooked eel approaches the bank. An eel is one of the most difficult fish an angler can ever hope to land. They are adept at curling their long sinuous tails around any underwater obstruction and stubbornly resisting the pull. They also have the ability to swim backwards – very unnerving to an inexperienced angler. They may even roll over and over in the water when hooked, causing the line to tangle which shows up any weakness or abrasion in it.

RIGHT: The archetypal eel water: old, serene and secluded. This lake is separated from the river by more than a mile of small streams and ditches and contains many large eels. The eels make their way into the lake as elvers and will stay for years until they feel the urge to return to the Atlantic to spawn. Whilst in the lake they feed on small fish, eggs, fry, water insects and invertebrates. In fact, the diet of the eel is as catholic as that of any freshwater fish species.

Anglers have long realized that eels have a very strong sense of smell. Their nostrils are elongated into short nose tubes and these run on either side of the upper lip. These tubes carry the smell of possible food items to the olfactory chamber situated within the nose. Eels feed off living or only just dead prey, such as bloodworms, fish spawn, a dying swan mussel, an incapacitated perch slashed by a pike's teeth, or even a drowning land animal. Food that is long dead and rotting can be identified by the eel's sharp sense of smell and will be rejected. It is true that eels are often plentiful downstream of slaughter houses where they may have taken to a diet of dead meat but it is more likely that they are feeding off the midges, insect lavae and worms that are abundant in the enriched water. As far as the angler is concerned, it is vital to make any bait not only smell as much as possible but also to smell as fresh as possible. Here is how it can be done.

If you are using a big bunch of worms as bait, snip off a few tails here and there or even puncture the bodies a little so that the scents drift out into the water. When deadbaits are on the line, puncture them with a sharp knife so the smell of blood, organs and stomach contents waft through the water. Change baits frequently so the smell remains strong and the offering on the hook does not become washed out and unattractive.

More advanced techniques of splicing up eel baits include injecting dead fish with concentrated oils. You could try some of the thousands of flavourings that are available on the carp fishing market. Many of these simulate blood or meat flavourings and can be sprayed on to the deadbait, injected into it, or brushed along the flanks of the bait. I find that 'Monster Crab' flavour is particularly successful when injected. However, do be very careful with the syringe when injecting bait as the accidental injection of an air bubble into your own bloodstream can prove fatal. For this reason, store the syringe with a needle guard on it and always inject the deadbait on a hard flat surface away from your fingers.

Finally, consider using a large swimfeeder when eel fishing and pack it with anything that smells of fresh blood: the guts of fish are an obvious choice but a simple piece of foam or sponge soaked in blood is equally effective.

it's useless after the first quarter. Late August to mid or late October is the season. A stormy night is good: a really wet one when the river is rising fast. If you watch the moon and the weather you can be exact about it and never miss. What I do sometimes nowadays is to set my fyke nets upstream of mills at night at the right times. This is a bit risky though, because there's so much rubbish coming down the rivers today. The other problem is that the water mills have been sold off as private houses. If there are lights on and music playing then the eels just won't run that way at all. Deadly sensitive to light eels are, but especially so when they're running.

'The Full Moon is absolutely useless and even when it's masked by cloud you don't get a thing. I've noticed that the eyes of silvers get larger and the pupils are so big that they can take in light even deep down in the sea. Perhaps the glow of the moon or houses or torches just dazzles them somehow.

'Mind you, night is always the time for eels, especially when the weather has been hot and humid. Round here, where there are lots of small roach and bream, my eels have big wide fish-eating heads which they develop from an early age. At night, when the pike are quiet, they will hunt the roach shoals in open water and hit into them like an explosion has taken place.' (Nocturnal bream anglers will testify to huge splashes in the water at night.)

'There are some waters round here that have lost their populations of small fish, generally through pollution of some sort from the land or the villages. But that doesn't stop the eel growing big and in such waters they just live off daphnia or hatching flies, like roach or rudd do. It might be my imagination, but the heads of these eels are more delicate, shaped for digging into mud or weed.

'The very biggest eel I ever saw in my life was in a pool like this, where it was all alone but for a few carp. The place dried up and I was told of a fish or two that had been left stranded in the mud. I went to investigate and I rescued four old carp, which I put in the village pond. I returned and right down there in the mud was this old monster. I brought it back and measured it here on this very table where we sit now and I swear it was sixty-two inches long. I didn't have scales to weigh it though, or a camera. I would like to be able to show you a photograph, because I don't suppose any of you will ever believe me. He was a poor beaten up

PREVIOUS PAGE: Just as the sun begins to set the eels become active and this is when the specialist eel angler sets out for a night's fishing. If the temperature dips a little the fish will be stimulated into feeding thus creating excellent fishing conditions. The shallow bays in the picture are good locations to fish in as the eels will drift in looking for food in the fertile water. The only problem that the eel fisherman may come up against is the temperature dropping too quickly. Eels, like all fish species, need a certain amount of stability in their environment and rapid temperature changes do not suit them.

sort of old sod, covered in scars and wounds that had healed up. I suppose things had got worse for him as the water dropped and the herons could have a go at him. Mind you, I should think any bird would have been scared to death of getting it wrapped round its throat. It probably didn't weigh as much as you think, because it was quite thin, like a broom handle. It had probably eaten everything else in the water and was left there, just hoping for a frog or a vole or something to swim past.

'I often get wrong with the anglers when they see me haul out my fyke nets, but I do everything right and I believe that I do them a good turn. If you've got too many eels in a water then all they will do is eat the eggs and the fingerlings and the fish populations will suffer. They'll even die out in some cases if there aren't enough successful spawning sessions to compensate. I reckon that by netting the eels out I allow the fry to grow into fingerlings and into small fish and keep all the anglers happy.' (Specialist anglers, after bigger quarry, might not be too pleased about this.)

'People like me get a bad name because of the cowboys. These characters know nothing much about eels, not much about nature and not much about anything apart from how much money they can make. They get up to all sorts of bad practices and often poach waters where they are not allowed. Another bad thing is to leave the net in the water day after day, perhaps even a week, without drawing it in and then you find all sorts of birds and animals caught and drowned. If you lay it at sunset and draw it in again before sunrise, then you won't get birds but just eels. These new blokes on the water will strip an eel population. They've got no thought for anything but quick cash and no view of the future, whatsoever. I also know for an absolute fact that there are men round here that take carp and tench – though they're not supposed to – and then sell them. There's no wonder that if anybody sees an eel fisherman doing that sort of thing we all get a bad name. I swear to you that every other type of fish that I've ever caught in all my life has gone straight back into the water.

'When I catch my eels I take care of them and treat them right and they can live for weeks and weeks. There's a lot of rubbish around that you can do almost anything to an eel and it will survive, but these are old wives' tales. For example, if you leave them in a bucket with not enough water, then they'll drown in their own slime, poor sods. I've caught eels that have been starving and found anglers' hooks in their throats. These chaps just cut their lines and think that somehow the eel will get rid of it. No chance. The eel goes away, can't swallow and soon begins to die of starvation. You find these eels with big heads and wasting bodies and nine times out of ten that's what's happened to them. A blow to the head will kill an eel as well, not instantly, but in about four days or so. They'll just creep off into some hiding place, an old sunk car wreck perhaps, and just slowly fade away and die. The life of an eel is a hard one and if they're going to get big and make it to old age, they need all the luck and wiliness they can get. I respect them for that. That's why they've got such sharp hearing and eyesight and a little brain in there that registers absolutely everything that's going on around it. Yes, I respect them all right, not that I really like them, but they've earned me a decent living. I've got a fair bit of money stashed away under my mattress, for when I decide to give it all up. And it's all down to eels.'

Next morning at dawn, we rowed out again across the placid Broad to where we had laid the nets the night before. Sure enough, there were no birds entrapped in the fine nets. The half-a-dozen tench we found in the sock end were released with the greatest possible care. All the eels were shaken from the net into two big tubs. These soon became a writhing mass of eel: at least a hundred-and-fifty fish, averaging a pound or so in weight. As we rowed back, I was really anxious that the boat would go under with the load, but we were fortunate that the wind didn't get up. There was barely a ripple as we made our way home and into the dyke by the cottage.

PREVIOUS PAGE: Loch Ness remains the most mysterious of the great freshwater lakes in the United Kingdom. No one knows its secrets, if, in fact, it has any. Ness looks so large and brooding that the imagination is bound to be fired by it. Centuries of legends do not help rational analysis either. We know that Ness is relatively barren, with limited food stocks and yet we all love to imagine that monsters exist in it.

June. Loch Ness on the bay below Drumnadrochit. The weather is very mild, with a wind blowing in from the south-west. The following relates the events of the fifth night in a series of seven. The other sessions were totally unproductive

Christopher Bennett has a penetrating piscatorial mind. It was he that first realized that porbeagle sharks might follow the Gulf Stream and visit the western and northern shores of Scotland throughout the winter. Putting his hunch to practical test, he risked day after day out in a small boat on the stormy seas off Cape Wrath and was finally rewarded with the British record porbeagle shark of over five hundred pounds. It is hardly surprising then that living just twenty miles from Loch Ness, he might be a little curious as to what might live there. It wasn't 'Nessie' that he had in mind, for Chris is not given to fantasy. The monster story, he suggests, is probably simply a heady brew of myth, suggestion and the occasional visit to the loch by a seal or even a sturgeon. No, Chris had taken an interest in the eels of Loch Ness and this had been prompted by some strange stories.

There is a power station on the south shore of the loch at the village of Foyers. Some years ago, two enormous eels had been found there, trapped in the screens that prevent rubbish from entering the turbines. Today, none of the locals remembers anything of those two creatures, though smaller eels are still found in the power station debris traps, from time to time. Another tale involves the tragedy of a certain titled lady who fell out of a boat and drowned in the icy loch. Royal Navy divers had been sent down to try and find the body. According to hearsay, the divers encountered enormous eels, that frightened them so much that they would not return to renew the search, even on pain of court martial. Stories have even come out of the religious house at Fort Augustus. Some of the friars report having seen huge eels cavorting on the surface on still summer nights. All in all, there was enough there to stir Chris's curiosity.

Long before he considered spending a week by the loch, Chris questioned whether Loch Ness could possibly hold vast eels. There is certainly food in the loch: shoals of char; brown trout and small pike. A very large eel might even have a go at a dead or dying salmon kelt.

Chris weighed up the fact that Loch Ness is one of the coldest freshwaters in Britain. For most of the year, the main body of water hovers at around 4°C and even the surface layers rarely move much above 12°C to 15°C. Could the cold water retard or even completely suppress the spawning migration in some eels? A proportion of any eel population lingers longer in fresh water than the rest, putting off the ultimately fatal migration to the Atlantic. This is how some eels grow so very large. It is just conceivable that the frigid waters of Loch Ness exert some kind of permanent 'cold shower' effect on some of the loch's eels. If some *did* remain in the loch for long periods, at least food would not be a problem.

Then Chris was struck by other possibilities. The loch would be a sanctuary, for it would be impossible to fyke net the entire loch. Also, the physical habitat would suit a big eel since the sides of the loch are supposedly honeycombed with gulleys into the rock: perfect for an eel to live in for seventy years or more.

For his sojourn on the loch, Chris chose Drumnadrochit Bay on the north shore, under the forbidding outline of Urquhart Castle. In the absence of any other information, the bay would be as good a starting point as any. At least it provided some shallows, before the drop off into the abyss of the loch itself. But, how on earth does one make a start to fish a loch that is 36 kilometres long and plunges to depths of over two hundred metres?

There had been a good May in Scotland that year and the shallows at Drumnadrochit were 14°C and rising. Chris hoped that this warm water would stimulate eels into investigating the area for food. There was weed there also, which would provide ambush possibilities for hunting eels and also attract small trout and even char into the area, in search of insects. Above all, local lore had it that pike spawned in Drumnadrochit Bay sometime in April. If this were the case, it would not be unreasonable to expect that eels would follow them in to eat the eggs and to prey on the baby pike through the summer.

LEFT: There was a time when vast sturgeon like this one roamed British coastlines and even entered major rivers. What amazing sights they must have presented as they forged upstream, feeding on shoals of chub and barbel. Today, their range has narrowed considerably and the chances of seeing a fish like this in the Thames are slim. However, there are those that believe that the Loch Ness Monster, if it exists at all, is a sturgeon that entered the loch years ago and has existed there on a diet of char, trout, pike and salmon. Far-fetched? Well, we do know that sturgeon can live for well over a hundred years and so fish first sighted in Loch Ness in the 1930s would not even be middle-aged today!

ABOVE: Another fascinating visitor to British rivers is the shad, a herring-like fish which swims upstream in vast numbers every springtime in the Wye, the Severn and the Shannon. In fact, in certain areas they are known as the Mayfish. This fish is one of the smaller species of Britain's two shads, the twaite. The larger shad, the allis, may well be extinct by now. After spawning, the shad make their way back to the sea. Any sick, injured or exhausted fish drift into the eddies and backwaters where they are picked off by pike, heron, cormorant and otter.

Chris timed his assault carefully. Knowing that eels are particularly active on warm, humid nights, he waited until a period of such weather settled on the Highlands that was forecast to continue for nine or ten days.

The tackle he chose was suitably strong: 20-pound class boat rods, with lines to match. He would bait both sets of tackle each night with a freshly killed rainbow trout, mounted on wire traces in case of pike. He also decided to use up-trace bags of 'rubby-dubby' on each set of tackle, filled with fresh minced fish. The emphasis would be on *fresh*: nothing that had not been killed the same day would be used and certainly not as a hook bait.

Chris decided that he would fish from 21.00 each evening to around 05.00 the next morning. He would give this a try for seven nights, which was all the time he could spare. In any case, he was probably chasing fairy tales.

The first four nights were uneventful, but utter hell because of the infernal midges which filled the warm still air. He had one run from a small jack pike, which dropped the bait. Its teeth marks on the trout's belly were plain to see. But that was all. Much of the time he scanned the water through binoculars, but nothing showed.

On the fifth night, things were different from the start. At around 23.00, a big shoal of char moved in over the ledge and began to rise in the bay. Soon after that, there were some heavy splashes and Chris assumed that pike were attacking the char. This suspicion proved correct when a little later he landed his first fish of the vigil – a pike of just 9½ pounds. It was a lanky emaciated creature which he quickly returned. At about midnight, he had another run of a few metres, but the fish dropped the bait before he could reach the rod.

At 02.00, fish began to rise all over the bay, something that he had not witnessed before. Shortly before 03.00, eruptions of jumping fish moved slowly from left to right across the area he was fishing. A hunter of some sort was clearly on the prowl. At 03.15, Chris had his third run of the night. This time he was ready for it: striking before a metre of line had left the spool, while walking backwards to help set the hooks. The rod hooped into a semi-circle and he had to give line to a fish that didn't really run, but appeared to be writhing and jagging some fifty metres out in the shallow bay. Seven or eight metres of line had been taken over the space of a minute and he had made no impression on the creature whatsoever when everything went slack. The line had parted at the swivel and all that remained was a big bow-wave heading out towards deeper water. Dawn came and Chris packed up and went home, his mind in a turmoil. Could it have been a seal, an otter, a very big pike or a ferox or even, God forbid, a passing sturgeon, or dare one even suggest that this huge creature was an eel? To this day Chris has no idea and will not comment.

Sticking to his plan, Chris fished on for another couple of nights, but without further incident.

Chapter 6

Pike
The Search for Monsters

LEFT: This pike is on the prowl. It hangs in mid-water, eyes alert, using its fins to move slowly backwards and forwards. Pike spend a large amount of time lying comatose on the bottom allowing their food to digest. Here they might be mistaken for an old log or stone. This is helped by the accumulations of silt which they allow to build up around them. As hunger sets in the fish rises and cruises, scattering the shoals of prey fish.

IZAAK WALTON SLANDERED THE PIKE DREADFULLY FOUR hundred years ago. He called her the water wolf, the sworn enemy to all. But the poor old pike has probably always had a bad press. If a villager lost his ducklings, then the pike was surely the culprit and not the fox and should a bullock cut its nose, it would be the pike at the watering hole and not the loose wire in the field that was responsible. It was always a pike that drowned the dog, however strong the current or thick the weed. Even an eighteenth-century vicar claimed that his gashed foot was from a pike attack while bathing and not the result of standing on a broken bottle. Over the centuries, river keepers have waged constant war on the pike, persecuting her relentlessly for the supposed harm she does to stocks of trout and other fish. Even in more enlightened times, coarse fishers (who should love pike) have let them swallow hooks, gaffed them cruelly, then whacked them over the head and taken them home for the cat.

I have personified the pike as feminine, because it really is the big grandmother pike that the angler is interested in. She can grow huge: an absolute monster of a fish to behold, it is true, and she will certainly dominate the life of her immediate environment. But to paint her as some embodiment of evil is absurd, of course: the pike has a place in its environment as does every other creature. It just happens to occupy the top niche in its food web as an efficient and impressive-looking predator.

And pike are very efficient predators, both as effective hunters and efficient converters of the food they catch: twice as efficient as trout, incidentally. It has been well documented that pike do eat a catholic assortment of prey from time to time, including some pretty bizarre items. But forget the ducklings and water voles. These are only the most occasional snacks. Pike are principally and predominantly fish eaters. Live prey are their staple, but they will also eat dead fish whenever they can.

Pike are ambush hunters rather than chasers: leopards rather than cheetahs, if you like. They either lie in wait for a prey to swim by or cruise around very slowly, hoping to steal up on a prey. When the victim is within range, the pike accelerates in a short, blistering burst of speed. Few can escape, save perhaps the smallest and most agile fish. Pike will eat most other coarse fish, including other smaller pike. They are the main predator on larger freshwater eels (see page 113) and in many lakes, trout are their principal food. Scientists have shown that a captive 10-pound pike can survive and grow normally on just three-and-a-half times its body weight of food in a year. In the natural state, a pike's annual consumption is probably five to six times its own body weight of food. This is far less than some earlier wild estimates of the pike's food intake, which vested the pike with quite impossible gluttony.

The removal of large female pike from a water is, if anything, likely to have a detrimental effect on a fishery. There is good evidence to suggest that when this occurs, the first thing to happen is an explosion in the numbers of small jack pike. These would normally have been controlled by the big pike had they been present. A large population of small and medium-sized pike has a far more damaging effect on both coarse and game fish numbers, until the balance is redressed.

A great female pike is not the rampant creature that Walton had us believe. She eats only when hungry, to quite modest and calculable needs. The remainder of the time she rests, sometimes, in cold conditions, in an almost comatose torpor. In shallow waters it is possible to find large pike in this condition. They will often make for quiet reedy areas and lie, like submerged logs, for days on end. They move so little that if a strong wind stirs up the silt and lays it finely over them, they will not even flick a pectoral to shift the sediment. A big pike on the bank is equally quiescent. It is tempting to think that she is aware of her fate and knows the game is up, but much more probable that the weight of her huge body out of water makes vigorous movement impossible. This is in sharp contrast to the frantic leapings around of small jacks.

As she lies there, perhaps on the frosted grass or on a bed of russet autumn leaves, any serious angler or student of nature finds her a lovely creature. Her belly is porcelain white, while the rich green and yellow markings on her flanks may be shot with flecks of orange. This wonderful mottled coloration provides the camouflage she needs to hide amongst the reeds and ambush her prey. Each fish has unique markings and these can be used to identify individual fish. The shape of a pike is always just perfect for that jet-like acceleration when she lunges at her prey.

It is the head of a pike that is so striking and unforgettable. The large, pitiless eyes are set high on the head for forward and upward vision. Pike have excellent vision, but even those occasionally blinded by cataracts can manage to eke out an existence. The fish has very sensitive organs in the skin for detecting vibrations and can locate prey by this means. The shovel-shaped mouth is enormous, both long and wide. It can open so massively that the fish can engulf prey of more than a third the fish's own body weight. In fact, a now famous sequence of photographs shows a three-week-old completely swallowing another three-week-old pike of the same size! Normally, however, a pike's preferred meal size is between 10 and 15 per cent of its own weight.

That terrible maw compels a closer inspection. The bottom jaw is rimmed with long piercing teeth, with razor-sharp edges (the reason pike anglers must use wire traces). The roof of the mouth is a forest of smaller needle-sharp teeth, all angled to point slightly backwards. The whole arrangement is perfectly designed to seize and hold a fish prey. That any fish can ever escape such a dreadful bite is quite amazing, but some do, as reservoir trout anglers can testify. A pike usually seizes its prey broadside, across the body. When the prey is subdued, the pike rearranges its position with a series of violent gulping actions, so that it can be swallowed head first.

To capture a really large female pike is one of the great goals in angling, but just how large do they actually grow? Some fifteen years ago, the great pike angling historian, Fred J. Buller, published *The Domesday Book of Mammoth Pike*. This massively researched tome recorded scores of fish over thirty-five pounds. The largest fish in Buller's catalogue of monsters was an incredible, but unverified $90^{1}/2$ pounds! The accepted current world rod caught record is a fish of 55 lb 1 oz, caught from Lake Grefeern, Germany in 1986. The current British record is a 46 lb 13 oz fish from Llandegfedd Reservoir in Wales, caught in 1994. Larger fish than these have been caught by other methods, or have been found dead. Several notable large still waters in the British Isles are capable of producing enormous pike and many believe that the existing record could be shattered (not merely broken) by some fish in the future.

RIGHT: This 47-pound Swedish pike held by its captor, Johnny Jensen, is probably the most dramatic fish I have ever seen. I remember thinking that its eyes were the size of sheep eyes and that its skin was ridged like an old oak tree. This vast female had entered a bay off the Baltic Sea to spawn and also to feed on shoals of roach and perch.

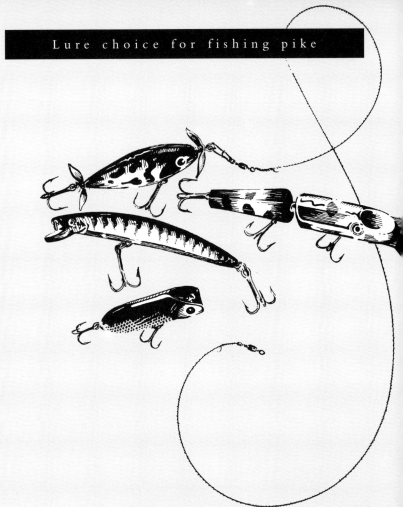

Knowledge of pike behaviour under various conditions is important when choosing the right sort of lure and knowing how to fish with it. When the water is warm pike tend to be in the shallow, reedy, bay-like areas and a floating plug is needed to reach the fish without constant weeding problems. There are many top water plugs on the market but probably the best have propellers both front and back which churn the water up and attract fish from metres away. Remember, too, that when the water is warm the pike are at their most active and a fairly brisk retrieve will attract and entice them into an immediate smash take.

When the water becomes colder, pike begin to move out of the shallows and into deeper water where they can be reached with a diving plug. These often float at rest but dive once the reel is cranked and will keep going down until the reel stops turning. It is a good idea to build up a selection which work best between two and five metres down. Remember to move these more slowly than you would a surfaced fished lure, allowing many pauses during which the plug will begin to rise tantalizingly in the water. Keep thinking as you work the plug in and try to impart some life to its movements either by varying the retrieve speed or by moving the rod tip from right to left.

When the weather is very cold the pike will go deeper still and now is the time to use a sinking plug which will descend to depths of ten or twelve metres. Use a large plug because a pike at this sort of depth will be hard to rouse and it will not want to expend energy on a small meal. This big plug must be worked as slowly as possible at depth: you are trying to pull the plug almost into the pike's jaws as it certainly won't be moving, chasing prey in these conditions.

Pike's eyesight can be sharp, especially in clear water. Think carefully when choosing the colour and finish of your lure. Are you trying to imitate a natural prey fish or attract a pike by flash? When imitating, light colours should be used in bright conditions and dark colours when the weather is cloudy. Fluorescent colours are useful in murky water especially if they mimic their surroundings, for example, fluorescent green shows up very well when the water is stained by algae. At night when the lure is silhouetted against the sky, black lures work better than anything else.

Finally, when choosing the right lure, it's best to use one that sends out the strongest possible vibrations. The pike has a highly developed ability to sense other fish in the water long before it can see them. It does this through its nervous system. A system of sense hairs and cells lies just proud of the epidermis. These pick up fish-like vibrations through the water and transmit messages to the fish allowing the pike to position itself for a successful attack. This vibration sensing apparatus also enables pike to attack their prey no matter how cloudy the water.

Summer. I am in a small boat on the Baltic Sea, two miles off the coast of Sweden. It is a clear day and a brisk warm wind is blowing from the south. Karl is a professional boatman. He lives in the village that is just visible between the islands, its gaily painted white and red houses vivid in the sunshine. Karl lets one or two small summer cottages to visitors, but his income comes mainly from taking out parties of anglers to troll for salmon and sea trout. In spring, he takes guests to fish for big pike, which come into the bays to spawn. In summer, they catch pike out in the sea itself. It was on just such a day, a few years back, that Karl landed his own largest pike from the area. It weighed a shade over fifty pounds and he has no doubt that these fish can easily reach sixty pounds or more.

These Baltic pike fascinate me, especially as a British angler who has trouble coping with the fact that the pike can actually live in salt water. Fishing for pike with trawlers and tankers going past is a strange experience, but when a pike is brought to the surface festooned in seaweed, with a crab dangling from its dorsal fin, the sensation is positively weird.

The behaviour of these Baltic pike is interesting. As soon as the winter begins to recede, they move from the sea two or three miles inland to their traditional spawning grounds. The same big fish go to the same bays, season after season, and individual fish can be recognized in the shallows. The migration is leisurely, taking several days as the fish wait for the water to reach a certain temperature before they are willing to enter the extreme shallows. On the way, they will certainly eat roach, perch and ide if they come across a shoal. After spawning, which takes place in late April or early May, these monstrous fish move back out to sea.

For most of the year, the pike live around submerged reefs and offshore islands. These features offer the fish some shelter from marine currents and provide lies from which the pike can ambush their prey, which are also attracted to the reefs and shallows around the islands. As in fresh water, the prey of these marine pike are mostly shoal fish. Herring and cod are most favoured, with the herring running to a pound or more and cod being taken of four or five pounds. The pike here also eat burbot, a fairly large eel-like member of the cod family, which used to be quite common in a few English rivers until its demise in the 1960s.

The Baltic is frequently stirred by wind and can become quite turbid. In murky water, pike cannot hunt effectively by sight alone. Their

PREVIOUS PAGE: The magnificent Lough Mask. This huge water has produced some of the most magnificent pike in history and, if left alone and not netted, will surely do so again. Its size and its fertility combine to produce pike of an almost unparalleled size.

whole body is a network of nerve endings which the fish uses to locate their prey.

Karl is probably right about the size potential of the Baltic's pike. The environment clearly suits them and it is stable and largely constant except for seasonal changes. Food is abundant and the prey fish grow large. What is more, the extent of the water is so vast (compared with inland lakes) that a large fish might easily avoid capture while it grows still larger. Anglers represent probably the greatest impediment to a pike realizing its growth potential, but in the Baltic Sea, overfishing is highly unlikely.

One can imagine one of these Baltic leviathans, possibly a metre-and-a-half long, lying in a rocky gully amidst waving fronds of seaweed. Her remarkable nervous system picks up the signals of a passing shoal of cod. As the fish move into view a target is selected and, with a lunge of breathtaking acceleration, she seizes a five-pound codling across the back. Returning to her lair, the feebly struggling codling is repositioned and gulped down head first. The meal will probably keep her satisfied for a week or more, depending on the water temperature. During this time, she will rest quietly, rocked by the Baltic currents amongst the drifting seaweed. What every angler hopes for is to be present when her hunger begins to stir, perhaps trolling a really large plug behind a slow-moving boat. As the lure slowly trundles along, its vibrations send out a siren song. Perhaps it will pass close enough for the hungry predator to lock on to the target and make the lunge that will be her downfall.

Loch Oich in Scotland. One April sometime in the 1950s. The scene is the shallows around the inflow of the River Garry on the north side of the loch.

Jock McGaskill was one of the best loved and most feared of all the gillies in the West of Scotland. He could be irascible, but once he came to know you, he would prove a true and loyal friend. The story he told rang with absolute truth. It dates from the period when he was involved with netting the waters of the Ness system for pike. In those days, pike culling operations were conducted annually, in the belief that this would improve the salmon and trout fishing. One spring in the 1950s, he was netting the shallow weedy area of Loch Oich where it is fed by the River Garry and where Pike were known to spawn here in numbers. Jock was very used to catching big salmon, but the pike he pulled into his boat one morning made him gasp. It was so large that he decided to take it back home to weigh it. The fish proved too heavy for his scales, even though he used them for weighing large salmon. In order to get its weight, he cut the fish in two and weighed the halves separately. They totalled between fifty-one and fifty-two pounds. It was hard to be exact because some of the stomach contents, eggs and blood had escaped in the severing. If Jock and his scales are believed, then the fish was certainly huge and gives an added credence to many of the other tales of Scottish leviathans.

Everything about this tale is plausible. There is no surprise that a big female pike should have been in the shallows at spawning time. She would have been there to spawn and to feed on the small jacks. Her size would surprise many but, once again, she would have found in Loch Oich the most important factors to sustain her enormous weight. Food supplies there are abundant. As well as jack pike, there are shoals of char in the system, especially if she moved west into neighbouring Loch Lochy. Salmon and even a few sea trout are present and after their winter breeding, the spent kelts would provide her with easy pickings. There is little doubt that she would have eaten trout and even a decent-sized ferox would have been within her capability if it got too close. And the topography of Loch Oich would also suit a giant pike. Its many small islands, shallow reefs and rocky gullies, provide a variety of potential ambushes for a large predator, while its deep water would offer sanctuary during her periods of digestive torpor.

Oich is a large water itself, several kilometres long, but it also offers access to Loch Lochy which is colossal. This great pike would have had an enormous range of water available to her had she chosen to use the connecting rivers and channels of the system. So the fish could move in deep water or in shallows, in still water or in a current. There is possibly no more stable an environment in the British Isles nor one that could offer a big fish more options or more security. It was just her bad luck

ABOVE: Pike tend to mirror their environment physically. Here a Scottish pike is being returned to a water low in food. The pike's slim, torpedo-like shape allows it to move quickly through the water to prey on small quick-moving brown trout and large shoals of char. There are few easy pickings for a pike in a Scottish loch and it could not support a heavier, more cumbersome shape like that of a trout-fed pike from an abundant reservoir.

LEFT: A break for lunch on one of the tranquil islands on Lough Corrib before the fishing recommences.

 that she swam into Jock's net in the shallows that night. Had she remained free, she might very well have grown even bigger, eventually to die somewhere in obscurity, perhaps even weighing sixty pounds or more.

Llandegfedd Reservoir, in South Wales. An overcast autumn day with a mild wind pushing in from the west over the 400-acre water.

Peter Smith was alternating between fishing lures and deadbaits from his boat some 150 metres off the famous north bank, where some of the largest, fully authenticated pike ever caught in Britain have been captured. He was feeling a constant yet suppressed excitement for, even though the fishing had been very slow, recent history had proved there were forty-pounders in this water and he was now fishing over one of their favoured zones. Pike do roam in trout waters like this, but the fact remains that most are caught in the same general areas. This is largely because prey fish gather in certain areas and these become known to the pike who soon adopt special feeding patrol routes.

Prey fish often give away the presence of a feeding pike and at around 11.00 that morning, a knot of rainbow trout broke the surface close to Smith's boat, scattering in obvious panic. Putting on his Polaroids, Smith stared down into the gloomy water and a pike swam slowly into his field of view, a little way below the surface. She was a huge fish, a veritable crocodile. For two minutes the pike remained in sight: long enough for the angler to gauge her length by comparing it against parts of his boat and, even, the handle of his landing net. Such measurements are obviously very rough and ready and lack any scientific precision, but Smith is sure that the fish was between forty-five and fifty pounds. Snapping out of his trance, he carefully lowered a dead smelt down towards the fish's nose. The alarmed pike immediately dived, leaving a boiling turbulence on the surface.

Llandegfedd Reservoir is the most notable example of a fairly recent phenomenon. In the past few years, reservoir trout fisheries have produced a remarkable string of enormous pike. Quite why the pike in stocked rainbow trout fisheries grow so large and so quickly is the subject of much discussion amongst pike anglers. A thirty-pound plus fish from a reservoir like Llandegfedd might be only seven or eight years old.

The first thing to realize is that most of these waters hold large stocks of coarse fish. The trout make up only a small percentage of the overall fish population in such a water. In the case of Llandegfedd, the coarse fish of all species grow very large indeed, so the water is clearly rich and has a natural capacity to produce outsize specimens. There is no doubt, however, that the rainbows do form part of the diet of Llandegfedd's big pike. When newly stocked from the holding pens, rainbow trout tend to swim around in shoals. They are naïve and vulnerable to start with and it takes them a few days to acclimatize to life in open water and having to fend for themselves. For the first few days at least these 'stockies' make an easy and nutritious addition to the pike's normal menu.

Waters like Llandegfedd are principally trout fisheries (often with only fly fishing allowed). Very little fishing pressure will be directed at the large pike resident in these waters. Moreover, these waters are relatively large and the pike have plenty of space in which to conduct their affairs. While pike are large and aggressive looking, they are not, in fact, particularly hardy. Fishing pressure is probably far more detrimental to the growth potential of pike than is generally appreciated. It is this comparative lack of angling directed against them, that allows the pike to attain such huge sizes in waters like Llandegfedd.

Smith didn't catch his fish because he is an incompetent angler. In waters with such an abundance of food, the pike are supremely well fed and can afford to be fastidious. Moreover, in such clear water the pike's excellent vision will allow it to scrutinize the bait carefully and detect anything unnatural. It is not unusual to witness a pike inspecting a bait from very close range for several minutes before making a decision. Sadly for the angler, that decision is often a negative one.

A year on Lough Mask, County Mayo in the West of Ireland. Mask is a huge rich water of some twenty thousand acres. It is shaped like an elongated triangle, some ten miles long and four miles wide at its broadest point.

Historically, Lough Mask has been the most productive water for large pike in the British Isles. According to Fred Buller, in *The Domesday Book of Mammoth Pike*, Mask had accounted for twenty-four fish of over thiry-five pounds by the mid 1970s. That is an extraordinary record for one

LEFT: A huge pike taken from a large, crystal clear lake is held for the camera before being returned to the water.

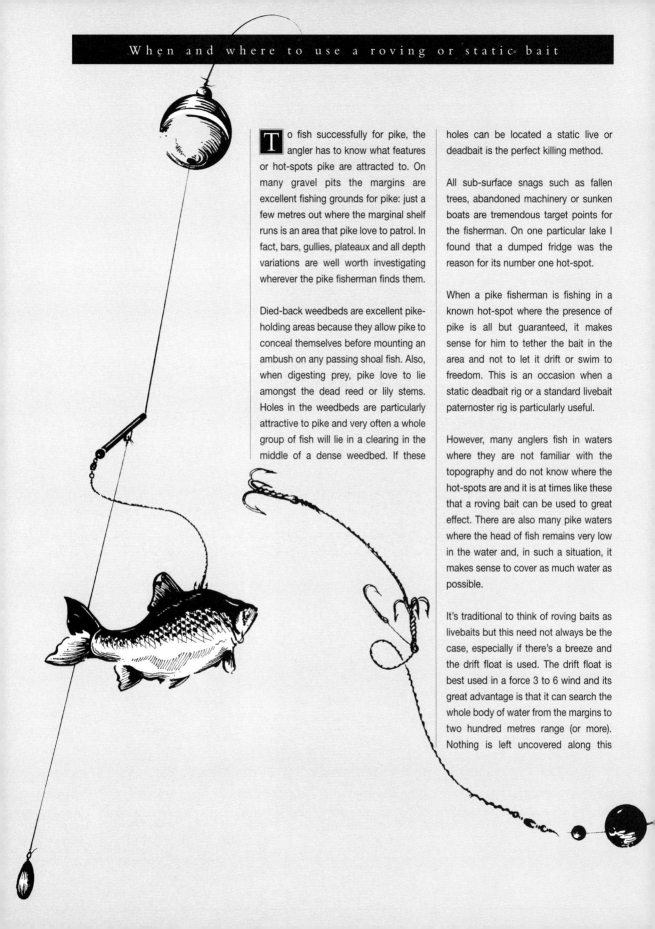

To fish successfully for pike, the angler has to know what features or hot-spots pike are attracted to. On many gravel pits the margins are excellent fishing grounds for pike: just a few metres out where the marginal shelf runs is an area that pike love to patrol. In fact, bars, gullies, plateaux and all depth variations are well worth investigating wherever the pike fisherman finds them.

Died-back weedbeds are excellent pike-holding areas because they allow pike to conceal themselves before mounting an ambush on any passing shoal fish. Also, when digesting prey, pike love to lie amongst the dead reed or lily stems. Holes in the weedbeds are particularly attractive to pike and very often a whole group of fish will lie in a clearing in the middle of a dense weedbed. If these holes can be located a static live or deadbait is the perfect killing method.

All sub-surface snags such as fallen trees, abandoned machinery or sunken boats are tremendous target points for the fisherman. On one particular lake I found that a dumped fridge was the reason for its number one hot-spot.

When a pike fisherman is fishing in a known hot-spot where the presence of pike is all but guaranteed, it makes sense for him to tether the bait in the area and not to let it drift or swim to freedom. This is an occasion when a static deadbait rig or a standard livebait paternoster rig is particularly useful.

However, many anglers fish in waters where they are not familiar with the topography and do not know where the hot-spots are and it is at times like these that a roving bait can be used to great effect. There are also many pike waters where the head of fish remains very low in the water and, in such a situation, it makes sense to cover as much water as possible.

It's traditional to think of roving baits as livebaits but this need not always be the case, especially if there's a breeze and the drift float is used. The drift float is best used in a force 3 to 6 wind and its great advantage is that it can search the whole body of water from the margins to two hundred metres range (or more). Nothing is left uncovered along this swathe of water. Of course, the more intelligently the drifter float is worked, the better the results. For example, it pays to stop the flow of line frequently to make the float move either right or left before the wind. It makes sense too to stop a float for a while near any obvious snag like a protruding tree branch, island or bank of dying weed. The drift float is especially useful when fishing for big fish that are hiding from the anglers in the sanctuary areas of large waters. The pike is a surprisingly aware fish and after it has been caught or frightened a couple of times in a known hot-spot, it will move out of the normal casting range.

It is important to use a good-sized bait – live or dead – when fishing the drift rig: a pike will only expend energy chasing a moving bait if it thinks that chase will result in a satisfying meal. A small and difficult to catch bait would frequently be ignored. Clear water is also advantageous to the fisherman, because in cloudy water the bait can drift past the fish at speed without ever being accurately located. A take on the drift float at long range is immensely exciting; sometimes the float sinks, or stops dead,

or travels up against the wind. The best advice is to be alert and check any unusual movements. Binoculars help you to keep track of the float movements and to make that all-important early strike.

You cannot strike at two hundred metres range, unless you are using braid, as there is simply too much stretch on the line. The trick is to tighten down, walking backwards with the rod held high. The hook is pulled home not so much by the angler's efforts as by the weight of the fish as it bends its head into the hooks.

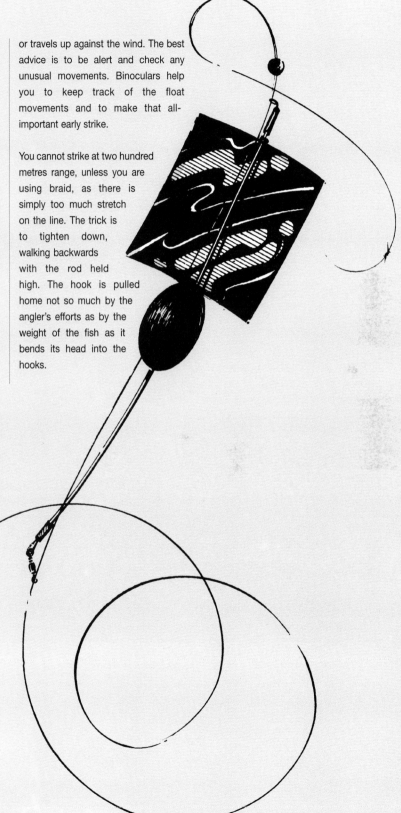

ABOVE: Two pike paired up in the preparation for spawning in the crystal clear shallows of Lough Corrib.

lake, especially when one considers that only ten such fish could be traced from the whole of Scotland and just six from the prolific Norfolk Broads. The supply of colossal pike from Mask has certainly not dried up, as a recent capture of a forty-two-pounder has proved. In fact, the chances of a true, wild fifty-pound pike being caught are nowhere higher anywhere in the British Isles today than from Lough Mask.

There is a shadow hanging over the water, however. Ireland's Inland Fisheries Board is threatening to resume pike netting on the water, trapping the big fish as they come into the bays to spawn. Not only are magnificent pike likely to be caught and killed in this purge, but almost certainly the number of jack pike will rocket if this cull goes ahead. If this occurs, there are many of the opinion that it would have a *detrimental* affect on the game fishing.

In fact, the pike population of Lough Mask is probably comparatively low. Most visiting anglers never even get a run, simply because of the sheer scale of the water and the difficulties in locating these sparsely distributed fish. If one is going to have any realistic prospect of catching a Lough Mask pike, one has to have a pretty good picture of where the fish will be and what they are doing at any particular time of the year.

Throughout January and February, pike fishing on Mask is slow as the fish become gravid with spawn. As breeding time approaches and with metabolic activity reduced by low water temperatures, the fish will not be moving around much. At this time of the year the fish are mostly found in areas of moderate depth, but close to the shallows. They will not chase a bait or a lure at this time, but may take a deadbait fished hard on the bottom around ledges and rocky outcrops.

During March, water temperatures begin to rise and the pike begin to move towards their spawning beds, often in water only half a metre deep. Weedy bays with lots of cover are favoured sites. Such shallow weedy areas absorb the warmth of the sun and will often be a few degrees warmer than the rest of the lough. These warmer patches of water not only attract the pike, but increase their metabolism and hunger. To stumble on such areas is a real find for the angler and can provide a most exciting experience. In these shallow bays, it is sometimes possible to wade quietly amongst pike preparing to spawn. Huge fish will cruise past, still hunting the smaller jack pike that are also gathering there for breeding.

In April and May, after spawning has finished, the pike are quite thin and exhausted by their procreative efforts. They need to feed and put on weight quickly. They will sometimes remain around the shallows after spawning, to hunt the numerous perch that are often present. Throughout June, July and August, the pike will be actively hunting as the water continues to warm. The perch will have spawned by now and move out of the shallows, closely tracked by the pike. In fact, at this stage in the year, once perch shoals have been found then the pike will almost certainly be in attendance.

September and October probably sees some of the very best and certainly the most beautiful fishing on Mask. At this time, the trout are starting their spawning run and heading towards the rivers which flow into the lough. If the rivers run high enough, the pike will actually leave the lough altogether, moving into fast currents to pursue the trout spawning on the redds. In many ways, this is the cream of Mask pike fishing, but it is soon over. Throughout November and December the water temperatures start to fall sharply and pike's metabolic activity slows down dramatically as a result. Once again, deadbaiting becomes the method most likely to produce a big fish and they will almost certainly be out in the deeper holes and gullies.

Men like Alan Broderick, David Overy, Frank Barbé and Richie Johnston know well the fabulous potential of Lough Mask. They are content to spend endless, cold, windswept days on the lough in search of its legendary pike. They have a list of thirty-pound-plus fish to their credit and in the summer of 1996 Alan caught a pike of almost forty-nine inches. Had he caught her in February or March, she would have been well over the forty-pound mark.

Chapter 7

Tench & Rudd
Peering into Pools

THE BEST ANGLERS SPEND AS MUCH TIME WATCHING WATER as they do fishing it and Polaroid glasses and binoculars are every bit as important as the tackle itself. By prolonged observation, these anglers gain an intimate knowledge and understanding of the waters they fish. For example, an area of clouded water in a lake might indicate a shoal of bream feeding early in the morning or in the late afternoon and the occasional sightings of waving black fins will confirm this. One leaping carp can herald a change in the wind, while the failure of a group of tench to appear on a particular shelf at their customary time in the early morning, could foretell a spell of poor weather drifting in from the west.

All the great discoveries in fishing have come about after hours of observation at close quarters and generally in very clear water. If the water is clouded, the failure to catch fish is not nearly so barbed. Under these conditions anglers can become complacent and perhaps won't really work at trying to discover their deficiencies. In turbid water, it could always be that the fish were elsewhere, or they weren't feeding that day, or any other plausible excuse to justify failure. But if the angler can actually see fish around his bait and feeding on it, and he is still experiencing no success, then serious questions have to be asked.

June 12th to July 9th 1987. Roger Miller devotes himself to Blickling Lake, a large estate water in Norfolk. Throughout the period, the weather is mild and temperatures are rising. In the sunshine, visibility is perfect into water as clear as air. Water temperatures rise, on average, one to two degrees each week.

11.30 June 28th. Miller packed up his rods in total disgust. Ever since opening day on June 16th it had been the same. Four hours earlier the tench had drifted into the swim, four metres out, and had begun to feed

LEFT: Blickling is one of Norfolk's most perfect estate lakes combining great natural beauty with extraordinary fertility. The water is clear for long periods over the summer and tench, bream and carp, among other fish, are often visible feeding on great banks of daphnia or extensive bloodworm beds. Although the fish are plentiful and large, catching them is never easy.

there. More and more fish had followed as the morning drew on and now he had forty fish in front of him, sucking up baits like a herd of miniature vacuum cleaners. Some of the tench were very big indeed. Miller had not had a single bite, nor had he for twelve mornings past and he just couldn't understand what had been going wrong. He cut a sorry picture, standing with his hands in his pockets staring moodily at the water, literally foaming with bubbles from the feeding tench. This really was a puzzle.

Despite disappointment at his failure, this mass of feeding tench was a wonderful sight and one that a fisherman/naturalist like Miller could easily appreciate. The fish were moving over a zone baited with particles of corn, maggots and hemp: tiny items of food that would keep the fish interested for hours. It was a mesmerizing sight as fish after fish glided over the carpet of bait, tipped slowly onto its head and fed for a minute, before levelling off and drifting away to chew what had been sucked into its mouth. Its place would then immediately be taken over by another member of the shoal. The pattern was repeated until the thousands of loose-fed particles had all been eaten and only Miller's hook bait remained, in splendid isolation on the sandy bottom. That very morning, these fish had eaten around ten cans of corn and a full bucket of maggots and hemp. Miller gloomily calculated that they must each be about a quarter of a pound heavier than they had been before their breakfast!

The swim was less than a metre deep and so clear that every grain of sand could be seen once the sun had risen over the oaks in the wood behind him. Morning after morning, Miller had watched this shoal of fish at their breakfast and had come to appreciate what order there was to their behaviour. The fish were totally unhurried, drifting gracefully through the water as if propelled by sub-surface breezes. Anglers have often commented on the beauty of tench: their tiny silk-like scales, the glow of their red eye and the sensual shape of their rounded fins, almost breast-like in the case of large females. To see them in the water like this, however, was an entirely different experience. For days, they had drifted like spirits: mahogany brown ghosts from the deeper water beyond. Yet, while Miller was capable of appreciating the magical dance that took place before him each morning, the whole thing was driving him crazy.

It had not been a complete waste of time, however, for Miller had learned a great deal about the fish. For example, the males and the females seemed to patrol quite distinct and separate territories. The males tended to be in larger groups of fifteen to twenty fish, whereas the larger females drifted in smaller sisterhoods of between three and six fish. There were also small groups of recognizable fish that travelled together morning after morning in tight little social groupings. He always looked out for one group of enormous females, that moved together in the most serene and unhurried fashion. There was always one noticeably darker fish at the head of this little group. She wasn't the largest, but she was certainly deeper in the body than her sisters.

There had been one period when this pattern of behaviour was interrupted. The weather had become very warm and the fish had taken a brief spawning interlude. The bulk of the spawning had occurred earlier in June, but tench do continue to carry eggs and milt throughout the summer and breed from time to time when the temperatures are particularly favourable. This spawning period lasted less than thirty-six hours, however, and within two mornings, the tench were back to their breakfast routine.

This morning session was quite obviously their main feeding period during the day and took place between sunrise and midday during warm periods, not at dawn as most tench anglers have been led to expect by various writers over the years. The lake is very close to the coast and cooling winds from the north spelt fast falling water temperatures at night which inhibited feeding until the sun had warmed the water. Sunshine and warm winds from the south or west were needed to stabilize truly favourable conditions. Around midday, the sun would become too bright for the fish in such shallow water and, one by one, they would tend to drift away into deeper water. By early afternoon the swim would be deserted.

Even within a fairly small swim, the tench favoured particular feeding places and one could clearly see where the silt had been totally removed by the fish excavating in their search for food. This particular morning, Miller gloomily reflected, the fish had created an even bigger saucer in the sand than usual: big enough for him to have buried his head in to forget his recent humiliations!

As he stood there, he turned events over in his mind. He had tried large baits, hoping that something different would attract a fish's eye and lure it into making a mistake. This proved quite useless. A piece of

RIGHT: Watching tench underwater is a hypnotic experience; they appear to glide effortlessly through weed and lily stems. You also realize how alert to tackle they are, particularly tackle that is clumsily presented. Here a swimfeeder lying on the bed is enough to alarm two fish, driving them to the back of the swim. Of course, here the water is crystal clear. If it were more cloudy their reaction might be very different.

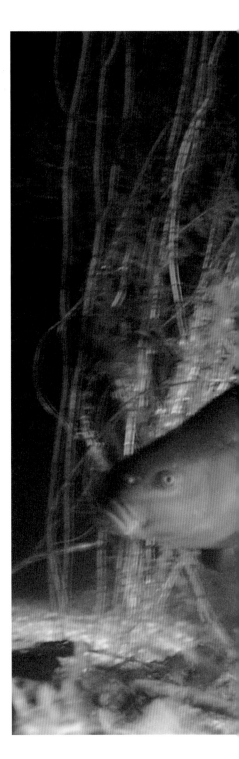

ABOVE: No wonder the tench is the favourite fish of so many anglers. Here is an impressive tench with beautiful scales and fins, startling red eyes and a powerful build. It it because of this muscular power that the tench puts up such a dramatic fight when hooked.

Even with the most cursory glance at a rudd's head it is impossible not to notice that big, protruding bottom lip which tells us that this is a fish used to taking its food from the water surface. Although rudd do feed on the bottom, they are happiest picking off rising nymphs and larvae hatching in the surface film and even fully emerged insects.

Rudd, however, are quite happy to tackle big baits too. The best starting bait for rudd is a piece of bread crust, the size of a ten-pence piece, if necessary, dunked in the margins to give it casting weight. For longer distances, a carp-type controller float can be used or even an old-fashioned bubble float. Bread crust is a particularly efficient bait at night when shoals of big rudd swim into the margins and suck and slurp under fallen branches, looking for moths and insects that have drowned during the day.

Once the floats send out warning signals that the rudd are feeding, move on to Chum Mixer biscuits. These are very popular on the carp scene but rudd also adore them; fish as small as half a pound have no trouble sucking them in. They must be fished soft, though, so measure out a pint of Chum into a plastic bag and pour a fifth of a cup of near boiling water over the top. Tie a knot in the top of the bag and shake until the water has covered all the biscuits. It will be absorbed gradually and at the end of this you will have nice soft baits which are easy to hook and easy for the fish to swallow. If necessary you can add either dye or flavouring at this stage as well: red is particularly effective in attracting rudd.

If the rudd are particularly wary, then they may only come up to feed on floating casters. This can, however, be a very effective killing method once rudd get the taste for them. Send about half a pint of casters out into the wind channel by catapult and then watch them, if necessary through binoculars, as they are blown down the lake or pit. As soon as fish are seen swirling beneath them, you can begin to fish. You will probably need a long cast for this. The perfect set-up is a 13-foot rod with a three pound line, a large waggler float and a size 16 hook. One or two floating casters on the hook should soon be taken. If the rudd are very cautious, then try sinking the last few centimetres of the line up from the bait or increase the distance between bait and float. Try to hustle any hooked fish away from the rest of the shoal as quickly as possible as rudd are probably the most easily spooked of all fish and the slightest sign of danger will cause the shoal to break up in alarm.

breadflake could be seen by a fish two or three metres away and sometimes they had even bolted from it! Clearly, tench had long memories. Blickling Lake has been fished heavily for a great many years and even as early as 1949, one writer had recommended large pieces of breadflake as the best bait there. Many of the fish that Miller had been watching were probably twenty to thirty years old. Perhaps some were even old enough to remember that particular author and what had worked with them in their youth was not going to fool them now in old age. On this lake, all the commonly used bread baits were identified as having dangerous associations and were avoided with real alarm.

In some ways, Miller could reflect that there had been a few successes. He had, after all, succeeded in weaning many of the fish off their natural diet of daphnia and other minute organisms onto food items that he could at least present on a hook. Several fish had become quite dependent on what he was feeding them every morning. He knew their territories and feeding times and had learned much about their behaviour generally. Indeed, he knew as much about tench as most and more about these particular tench in this lake as anybody … it was just that he couldn't catch them!

He had thrown the remains of a can of sweet corn into the shallows right by his feet and, to his amazement, a tench of around five pounds was sidling up to the grains, despite his very obvious presence looming above. It was maddening: the tench clearly knew he was there, but had decided that he no longer presented a threat. The fish was obviously still hungry and tipped on its head to begin feeding. So shallow was the water that its tail broke the surface and waved in a derisory fashion, as the corn was 'hoovered' up. Putting on his Polaroids, Miller squatted down to watch the action, literally in front of his nose. The fish was so close he could even have grabbed it by the tail and pulled it onto the bank. In his present state of mind, the thought was almost tempting!

Suddenly, Miller noticed something that he had not been aware of before. The fish was not picking up the bait with its lips at all, but actually sucking it in from an inch or so above the lake bed. No contact was being made. There was no doubt about it. The fish took five minutes to consume forty or so pieces of corn in this manner, then wandered away to rejoin its companions.

LEFT: Rudd waters are rare nowadays. Traditionally, rudd inhabited tiny pools and pits in unspoilt farmland but many of these waters have now been drained, filled in or polluted and rudd populations have suffered accordingly. Today rudd are found in these smaller waters only in extremely rural areas where building pressure is kept to a minimum. Other waters where rudd are present include large gravel pits dug after the War, which have had rudd introduced into them.

ABOVE: This is a stunning rudd – the sort most anglers only dream of catching nowadays. The bright golden scales, vivid red fins and dinner-plate shape are all indications that there has been no roach hybridization here. Roach and rudd do frequently breed together and this can lead to confusion, especially when records are being talked about.

Miller also decided to leave and as he walked alongside the lake to his car his thoughts were completely absorbed by what he had just witnessed. Why on earth were the fish feeding in this way? It then occurred to him that when fish were feeding on small items lying on the bottom, 'hoovering' them up in this fashion was probably far more efficient than picking them up individually between the lips. The fish simply opens its mouth, increases the volume of its buccal cavity and thereby creates a 'partial vacuum', which draws in the morsel of food. The sand, silt and bits of debris that are also sucked in are expelled through the gills. Miller was also tempted to believe that the fish might have developed this mode of feeding as a defence against anglers. Any bait that was unnaturally heavy – such as one with a hook in it – would resist being sucked up and therefore get left behind on the bottom. Perhaps this was the cause of all his frustration.

That night, Miller worked hard in his kitchen, inserting pieces of polystyrene into large grains of corn that he had selected and hollowed out with a needle. Once he had prepared a selection, he threaded them onto a variety of hooks and then tested them in a jar of water. What he was trying to achieve was an almost neutral buoyancy. It was a fiddly, time-consuming job, but at least when Miller retired for the night his hopes were high.

The next morning, he realized that his labours had been worth it. In four hours, his float dipped quickly three times and one fish was hooked, played and landed. That morning was a breakthrough. Miller soon realized that a short hair-rig would have the same effect as polystyrene-packed corn, as would three floating casters on a size twelve or fourteen hook. As long as the bait could be sucked up naturally along with the free offerings, the tench would take it. A major breakthrough.

There remained work to be done, however, for he was only catching a few fish and none of them were the really big females, who always seemed to be in a different part of the swim. So far, he had only managed to catch some of the smaller, more competitive males.

Just after noon on July 7th, Miller was about to pack up for the day, as the fish had departed the swim he was fishing. Suddenly, a big solitary female loomed over the shelf into the shallow water to the right of where his float was riding. The bright sunlight made observation easy as the fish meandered casually to within a metre of the bait where it slowed, stopped and then made a decided detour past it. On reaching the left side of the swim, the fish began to feed. Miller recast to within a metre in front of the fish, gauging its approach carefully. The fish stopped feeding and once again detoured off its chosen line, as though to avoid the tackle. Three more times Miller cast in front of the fish and each time the big tench took avoiding action, before disappearing into the deeper water. The only possible conclusion that Miller could draw from all this was that the fish was seeing the float, the line or both. It seemed to spot his end tackle at a range of about a metre, then take evasive action.

Over the following two days, Miller experimented with different float sizes, colours, materials and positions in the water, but none of this made any difference: the fish still clearly took exception to his tackle. He decided that the float had to go and the line had to be laid flat on the bottom if this problem were to be overcome.

On July 9th, at 11.50, a lone big tench once again drifted into the shallow water of the swim. First, it picked up a few scattered grains of sweet corn, then it approached Miller's hook bait. This time there was no float, just a lead tethering the line to the sand. The tench didn't seem to have noticed anything untoward as it hovered horizontally in the water for a good eight or nine minutes. It looked like a great brown log in the water and, as he watched it, Miller felt the sweat begin to bead on his brow. What was going on in the mind of this big fish and why was it taking so long to decide on the bait? Was the fish still hungry? Was it suspicious, watching and waiting for a grain of corn that looked somehow out of the ordinary to be removed? The tench, quite suddenly, inclined its body slightly and the corn was gone.

The big female tench put up an awesome fight in the weed-choked lake. Many times in the ensuing twenty minutes the fish buried itself in the vegetation and the line went dead and unmovable. Each time, to Miller's intense relief, the tench broke free of the weed and the battle was rejoined. Eventually, the fish was beaten and the sight of the great brown fish rolling towards the net brought an end to an extraordinary episode for Miller. The visitors to the Hall gardens half a mile up the lake heard his whoop of triumph.

ABOVE: Wild carp are the traditional fully-scaled carp that were introduced into this country after the Norman Conquest, in the eleventh or early twelfth century. They tend to be smaller than normal common carp, leaner and more chub-like in shape. Sadly, like the rudd, wild carp are a disappearing species, pushed out by development and by the introduction of a large continental carp population which has begun to dominate British waters.

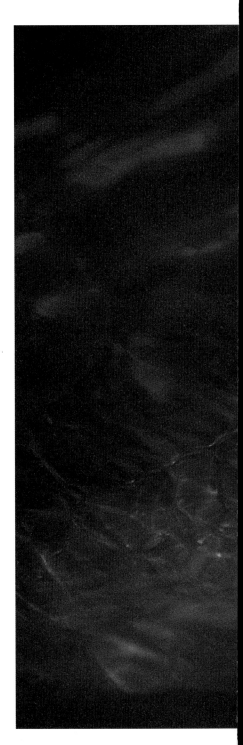

RIGHT: It is extremely rare for a crucian carp to be photographed so close to the water's surface but here is proof that what is generally considered a bottom fish will come up to the surface if conditions are peaceful.

The pool on Helsdon's Common in an August heatwave. The water is perilously low and clear and the weed growth luxuriant in this pond of barely half an acre. Air temperatures are up into the high twenties and the water temperatures are following.

The pond at the tip of Helsdon's Common is a very old one. According to farm records, it was originally dug in 1782 for marl to be spread on the land. Now it is overgrown and neglected: a repository for generations of village rubbish. Broken prams; bicycles and cracked pots; horseshoes; old plough shares; two tractor tyres and an engine block are its monuments to the passage of time. Despite this junk, there is a flourishing population of fish, stocked haphazardly by generations of farmers' boys.

Piscatorially, the pond is a page from the past. They are all old fish: the traditional, now unfashionable species that flourished in this country before the craze for modern imports, like mirror carp and catfish. Here there are still rudd and crucians, perch and even wild carp – the long, lean fully scaled carp brought to England by the Normans.

One strange thing is that the water is not fished. This is very unusual in these pressurized days when the anglers of this crowded island cast hungry eyes on practically any puddle of a water. Apparently, the rumour got around that the pool was polluted some years ago by a chemical spillage and had never recovered from it. As a result, even the village boys have kept clear of the place, often warned off by their parents fearful of some mysterious contamination. If the truth be known, the rumour started when a handful of bream found the stresses of spawning too much one year and died. A half dozen corpses floating belly-up in the margins was all it took: the pond clearly had the mark of doom upon it. In a curious way, these deaths were sacrificial, resulting in a respite for the other fish living in the pool. For some years they have been unmolested and now behave completely naturally. Watching them is like gazing into an aquarium.

I am fishing a small dead rudd a metre-and-a-half down on the bottom of the pool's deepest hole. It is intended for one of the passing perch, but I am not hopeful nor am I in a hurry. It's just an excuse to be here really, for I am quite content to spend the day watching: observing

Most anglers fishing on new water would start by using large traditional baits such as lobworms, bread and luncheon meat; all highly visible, extemely tasty and very attractive to tench. However, tench wise up quickly to obvious baits like these. As the bites begin to peter out, it is a good idea to lay a carpet of hemp beneath the fish to keep them browsing in the swim. This will allow you to use big baits again for a while before they are rejected once more.

Next move on to particle baits, which should be scattered over the hemp carpet. Start with standard yellow sweet corn and, when the bites die off again, try dyed or flavoured corn. At present there is the excellent Pescaviva on the market; a dyed and flavoured sweet corn which comes in an enormous number of varieties and keeps tench feeding on the bait for a long time. When the fish are behaving confidently, use two or three grains of this but as they become more cautious one or even half a grain should be enough.

When the tench are not responding to the corn any longer try using maggots or casters. Both are attractive to tench but casters have the advantage of lying still on the bottom whereas maggots soon creep into the silt or under stones. Use the lightest casters which will counteract the weight of the hook and produce easier to hit bites. Bunches of maggots and casters can be used at first. However, as the tench begin to spook use just one or two baits on a size 12 or 14 hook.

After maggots and casters, maple peas can be used as these work well for tench, especially when fished over the hemp carpet. To prepare the maples bring them to the boil in water with a couple of tablespoons of sugar dissolved in it. Simmer until they are soft enough to take a hook without splitting. Sprinkle a few maples on the hemp carpet (half a pint of maples is ample for a long tench session). Other excellent tench particles such as black-eyed beans, tares, peanuts and Aduki beans can be fished in the same way. Do make sure that all these particles, except corn or maggots, are well boiled so there is no chance of them swelling up inside the fish and causing them harm.

Most particle baits can be fished successfully on a hair-rig but when fishing tench it is important not to make this too long. For most situations a centimetre is about right. However, hair-rigs are fiddly to use and not always necessary. Very often scaling down the size of the hook a little works well. Do not make the hook too small though, as tench are tremendous fighters and will expose any weakness in the tackle immediately. The other alternative to using a hair-rig is to make the bait buoyant, for example by attaching a floating caster to a hook with two maggots as bait. Add a yellow grain of polystyrene to a hook alongside a piece of sweet corn to achieve the same effect.

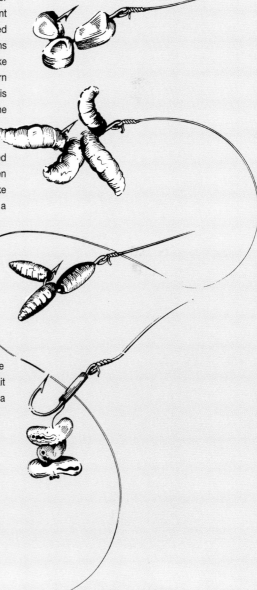

LEFT: There is no better indication of the presence of feeding fish than the silt cloud. Tench, carp, bream, even roach and rudd all stir the bottom up as they feed and betray their presence. In this instance a carp began feeding and a group of small perch moved in to feed on the bloodworm that it was disturbing.

 the life of a fascinating pool. The sun is well up and I can hear the growl of a tractor somewhere away over in the fields. Wood-pigeons are cooing in the nearby copse and the day promises treats in store.

It is the rudd that catch the eye first, so vivid in their reds and golds. There is a large shoal of around sixty fish, from perhaps a few ounces to a pound or even more: grand creatures for a puddle like this. Of all the freshwater fish in this country, the rudd is the most sadly neglected. It must be one of the most beautiful native fish we possess and yet we manage to ignore it. If the sparrow and the starling were heading for extinction there would probably be a public outcry but, as rudd numbers dwindle, nobody does a thing!

No fish could be more alert than the rudd, both to danger and to food. They seem to sense that they are small fish, ripe for persecution, and behave as true shoal fish, with a collective strategy against predation. Every member of the shoal is constantly aware of its immediate neighbours and the whole group squirts away instantly in a body when alarmed by anything. Carp or tench are much more confident and a group of them will mill around haphazardly, taking time to form into a body and flee should danger present itself. This is not so with rudd. If a pigeon flies over, casting a shadow, the shoal instantly zig-zags away into the weed in a tight phalanx with not a single straggler.

Food is of equal interest and the shoal patrols with its eyes constantly ranging from mid-water to the surface so that shrimps and water-boatmen are taken instantly if they are spotted leaving cover within a range of a metre or so. Craneflies blown off surrounding trees are slurped in by the bigger fish and a drowning wasp is pecked at by two smaller rudd until a fish of a pound appears and gulps it down with a gusto that suggests rudd do not get stung.

Rumour has it that just after the War the rudd here grew to two pounds and that there were hundreds of them. With the fall in the water table, however, the shallow area of the pond was reduced considerably and with it the available spawning beds. Another serious blow was dealt to the rudd by a local pike angler searching for livebaits. He netted the water one October and took away 150 fish which were wasted on waters as far away as Loch Lomond. A sad end for fish like these.

But where there is life there is hope and the wild carp are flourishing. The babies, last year's fry, are now about 12 cm long and spend all day sucking the reed beds, constantly kissing the duck weed and the cast-off shucks of the previous evening's midges. A slice of bread thrown away by the tractor driver at lunch time is dropped by a passing sparrow, drifts into the overgrown margin and is nibbled away for the rest of the afternoon.

The adults too, all twenty or so of them, are content browsing under the trees, taking the odd insect from the surface if the opportunity presents. They too fed heavily the evening before on hatching midge, when they could be seen nymphing like rainbows in a trout lake. In the early hours of the morning the group would have foraged for bloodworm, only easing off around 05.00 to spend the rest of the day largely at leisure. Old fish like this deserve their rest. I know the man who stocked them in 1945 or '46 and the same big fish have remained in residence ever since.

The crucian carp, however, have probably been in the pond for two hundred years. Certainly some of the old men in the village remember catching them as boys and taking them home in buckets on the handlebars of their bicycles, to stock in garden ponds around the parish. That pike fisherman with his nets did some damage to their numbers too, but fortunately the cold had come early that year and many were skulking deep down in amongst the tree and lily roots and so escaped the meshes. These are peculiar crucians, cunning pixies of fish that love to do everything possible to fool the fisherman. Today, a few of them are hiding away under the roots of the willows and alders and you can actually see their tails and heads poking out here and there, then moving and changing places with a neighbour.

There is one free-swimming shoal of crucians though: some of the big fish that seem to like swimming round and round the pond. They attack the floating bread that I throw in with glee. How many farmers' sandwiches have they gulped in over the years? And how many anglers would really believe that crucians are anything but bottom feeders, afraid of the sunlight and only moving from cover at dusk or dawn? A pond like this can teach a fisherman an awful lot.

There is only one shoal of perch in the pond nowadays, about thirty fish between 12 ounces and perhaps two pounds. I have always had the hope that there might be a solitary large survivor from the disease that struck here four or five years ago. What actually happened no one knows,

LEFT: *Fallen branches and weed are a sure sign that perch are around.. The dorsal fin of this fish is held proud and erect, a sign of an alert fish on the move, probably looking for a meal. That dorsal fin tells us a lot about the perch's mood: if it is lowered and sagging, then the perch is probably resting.*

but perch died by the score, suffering from terrible bleeding lesions that killed them within the day. All seems well now, thankfully, and the shoal looks as fit as a team of rugby players in their black-hooped shirts as they muscle round the pond looking for the action. Whenever they draw near, the rudd get distinctly apprehensive and take care to keep the bed of arrowhead lilies between them. Unabashed, the perch head for an old rusting rake head lying in half-a-metre of water where they all begin to scratch their bodies against the tines. Twisting and turning, they really scrape their scales over the rusting metal and seem to take a lot of pleasure from doing this. Abrasive ablutions over, the perch move off to grub about in the nearby weedbed. They are disturbing droves of water-boatmen, which are gulped down in the blinking of an eye.

While I have been watching all this activity, I have caught occasional glimpses of the pond's solitary large eel, snaking here and there around the water. It is well over four pounds and a conundrum in its own right. How on earth did it get here? It is at least four miles from the nearest water course and there are no drains, feeder streams or any other kind of conduit to this little pit, elevated even on a hill of gravel, sand and shingle.

Way back in the 1930s, some of the old boys here used to stock ponds like this with bucketfuls of elvers. They would leave them strictly alone for a few years to grow, then come back and net out the resulting harvest. Perhaps our slowly swimming, sinuous friend is a remnant of these? Or perhaps it arrived one evening, entwined around a heron's beak, refusing to be swallowed? It's a possibility: the bird shaking the eel off and it escaping, maybe wounded, into the pond. Here it recovered and grew large, a frustrated fish never to make that journey to the Sargasso Sea.

It is fair to assume that the eel is a 'her'. She would spend the midday hours entombed in weed, her head poking out into a little clear patch of water, made rusty by clouds of drifting daphnia. Rolling her eyes, and with a rhythmic swelling of her muscular throat, the eel gulps down the tiny organisms. Later, she stirs. The weed begins to shake and move around her and she sets off on a tour of the pool. Every time she swims through a sun beam, her body glows a sinister jade green. She too eyes the rudd and they know it. From time to time she hides in an old watering-can, curled up inside, her great broad head swaying this way and that, following the life of the pool.

Here I am sitting next to a truly cosmopolitan little community, where several different species exist together in close and interdependent society. There is a natural harmony to it: the sick and injured are consumed, while the most vigorous and healthy thrive, if warily, together. Of course, this microcosm is fragile and droughts are a constant menace. Nor would it need much to pollute a water so tiny: the dregs from a can of weed killer would do it. Unchecked water abstraction could turn the bed of the pond to a desert, or it could become a tip for farm rubbish. There is even a rumour current that the Chairman of the Parish Council – who happens to have a builder for a brother – is pushing for housing development on the field. Perhaps one day soon a chalet bungalow with all mod cons will sit happily upon the pond's grave.

It is eight in the evening now and an early heron makes its wheeling approach. It sees me, however, and flaps its way towards the north, croaking furiously. It's time for me to reel in as well, as the shadows lengthen and the life of the pool is gradually absorbed from my view by the dusk. I am really rather glad my dead ruddling had not been taken by a perch: in some way a privilege would have been breached. On such a glorious day it was infinitely preferable to be absorbed into the world of the pond: its colour, movement and life. To have pulled out a struggling fish would have been to lose all this to the spreading ripples.

Chapter 8

Roach & Grayling
Knowing the River

THESE SHIFTING RESIDENTS OF THE RIVER INHABIT A WORLD where nothing is ever static. The river never sleeps but is always cutting new holes, scouring its gravels and it may even change its course after a winter flood or sudden storm. In this world of flux, river fish are always on the move. The perch, perhaps, live in an eddy one week and then flit away to the pool beneath the bridge, or the one below the weir. Pike will also shift. Drought may push them out of favourite lies, or it may be because of angling pressure, or because their prey has moved elsewhere. The secret of all river fishing, therefore, is to read precisely where the shoals have settled and find out when exactly they come on the feed. With no species can this be more difficult than with roach or grayling.

Lowland river roach are a puzzle in themselves and they have suffered some serious set-backs in recent times. Since the Second World War, many of England's rivers have been subjected to dredging and canalization, mainly for flood control. This has greatly affected the environment of rivers and destroyed many natural holding places. From time to time, there have also been epidemics of fish diseases. The most important of these as far as roach are concerned has been columnaris. The disease causes great lesions and eats away at the scales and fins of the fish and can practically wipe out an entire shoal. It was against this inauspicious background that, in the 1970s, I set out in search of a monster roach: a fish so large that it would satisfy even my ambitions.

LEFT: This beautiful roach pool, surrounded by weed, offers deep, cool, clear water for a shoal of large fish. On many rivers, roach are highly localized and it is very important to explore as much of the river as possible to find the areas they like to inhabit. Bends, deep holes and large underwater snags all prove attractive.

 *October. The River Wensum in East Anglia. A typical lowland roach river, enjoying an Indian summer of warm days and mild nights. The river runs slow and clear and weed growth remains luxuriant.*

In those days I lived close to the river and it was no problem for me to rise early and be out as the dawn mists began to rise. On this particular occasion, I left the cottage at about six in the morning with binoculars, Polaroids and a loaf of bread. It was fish *location*, rather than fishing, that I was interested in that day. Since the 1960s, disease had significantly reduced the roach population, while dredging had altered their habitat enormously. So scattered were the roach in the river by then that one could fish for weeks without getting a bait anywhere near a roach. It really was necessary to go and find the fish. Fortunately, those fish that remained had not changed their habits. They could be relied on to give themselves away by rolling noticeably on mornings as still and serene as this, especially before the first frosts had begun to chill the water.

Why roach roll on the surface, no one quite knows. It is a magical sight: without a sound, the fish porpoises in effortless slow motion. The angler is fixed with an image of red finned silver, fading out in wide ripples. My own experience has always been that a rolling roach is a feeding roach and my pulse has always quickened at the sight. What these fish are not doing is taking insects or any other food off the surface. I have watched roach rolling from close enough on numerous occasions to be absolutely sure of that. My own guess is that the activity is an expression of tension, excitement even, that some of the shoal experience as they approach their feeding grounds. It is often noticeable that it is the largest roach in the shoal that roll. Perhaps it is some kind of signal for the rest of the shoal following on behind.

That particular morning, I made my way to the crest of a hill where I was able to see the river perfectly clearly for half-a-mile both upstream and down. Long experience has taught me that there is little to be gained in walking at water level and a good vantage point from which the river can be scanned extensively is far more useful. In the past, I had used trees or even a church tower but, on that day, the elevated knoll was just right for viewing a stretch of slow water leading towards an eighteenth-century mill.

I had learned to take things easy during these periods of reconnaissance. I knew full well that I might have to wait for two or three hours before a roach showed itself and betrayed the presence of a shoal. On many mornings, I went without seeing a sign of a fish and I had learned to choose only really mild, still mornings, when there was at least some chance of a sighting.

On this particular morning I was fortunate. At 07.10, heavy rings spread out just beneath a small island a quarter-of-a-mile upriver from the mill. I panned the area carefully with my binoculars, fearful that the commotion might have been that of a coot or a grebe. As there was no sign of waterfowl, I marked the position carefully against the bottom tree on the island and with rushes on the far bank and galloped off down the hill to investigate. As I crossed the flood plain my heart was in my mouth, praying that the fish responsible for the disturbance was really a roach and not a stray chub or pike. I was there in ten minutes.

From where I crouched in the reeds, there was no doubt what I was looking at three metres away. Another roach rolled, this time a very big fish and, like the Mona Lisa, seemed to look me straight in the eye. Over the next twenty minutes or so three other fish followed suit – all enormous! I was sure that none of them was under three pounds. I had set myself the target of three pounds as a personal bench mark in a quest that had lasted for more than a decade. At last I had found an area where some very big roach fed. And finding them was the most vital element in catching them.

It is important to realize that roach do not feed everywhere: they are not uniformly distributed along the river. Roach look for places where the gravel is cleaned of silt and weed or odd depressions have been formed, perhaps by a grubbing swan. There are many things that might be attractive to big roach as a feeding area: perhaps a glimpse of the chalk bed, or a slight narrowing of the river which deepens and speeds the water. Sometimes the bend of a river is chosen because of the depth and variation in the current. Rushes are often a magnet because they tend to store heat in winter, as do alder fringes which also provide shelter from the wind. Man-made features also play their part: old bridge footings perhaps, or weirs. However, nothing in my experience, before or since, matched this particular location in its consistent attraction for big roach.

I was back later that morning with the rod to plumb the depths. Upstream, the water was a steady one metre deep. Suddenly, within a rod's length, the river bed plunged to a depth of five metres. This deep

RIGHT: Roach fishing can take many different forms – from the angler sitting quietly on a bend hoping to mount an ambush to him wading the stream, trotting a float and exploring as much water as possible.

LEFT: When winter frosts begin to bite, roach swim miles from upriver down towards the bottom mills where the water is deeper, slower and offers them more food and protection. In East Anglia this pattern of movement has been recognized for more than a century. The fish generally begin to arrive around Christmas but if cold weather arrives before then, the downstream migration occurs much earlier. The fish only return upstream, looking for faster, more gravelly water at the beginning of April as they are about to spawn.

water extended right across the river, from bank to bank, and continued for around five or six metres downriver. Thereafter, the river quickly became shallow again and regained a steady one metre's depth again about twenty metres downstream. The sun was high and, with the help of polarized glasses, I could stare deep down into the river. On the bottom, I could see water-cabbages growing over a gravel bed, the former giving shelter and the latter providing a perfect dining table. Moreover, I noticed that the current of the river swept over this deep hole, leaving much slower water down in the trough itself. The swim was sheltered from the north winds by the trees on the island and from any cold snaps from the east by a stand of poplars. The only weather that would affect this particular place would be warm westerlies and these would do no harm to the fish or the fishing. Everything about the place spelt sanctuary, even floods would rush over the heads of the fish. Down in their deep trench they could feed undisturbed on the snails and shrimps amongst the water-cabbages.

I was thrilled by my discovery, for I knew that this if any was the roach swim that could give me my big fish. I was also puzzled. What had created this enormous depression in an otherwise featureless stretch of river? That afternoon, I went first to the city library, but my search there

failed to turn up anything. Then I went to the university and its History Department where I had friends. After a couple of hours I found what I was looking for. My deep trench was at the site of a Norman mill, recorded in the Domesday Book as Helsinga. It had been burned down in the fourteenth century, leaving just charred timber on the banks and that extraordinary, deep hole in the river bed. A new mill was built some centuries later a quarter-of-a-mile downriver from the earlier one, which was never restored. Helsinga was forgotten by everyone apart from the roach. Now it had been rediscovered by an ardent roach angler.

The next step was to wean the fish onto an angler's bait. The Wensum has always been a very rich river: a haven for snails; shrimps; caddis and corixae. With so little competition for food, the roach have always been suspicious of artificial baits. Nor had the stretch been fished for many years. Lonely and remote, it was considered next to useless after the ravages of columnaris virtually a decade before. What I now had to do was draw the fish in; condition them to expect the kind of bait I wanted them to eat and tempt them into my trap. This would not necessarily be easy. Even though I had found fish and a preferred feeding place, there were still very few roach in the river and those that there were had at least four miles of water in which to spread themselves about and hide.

As was my usual practice, I chose bread for bait. Roach adore the smell and taste of it, but more importantly, bread is a bait that the fish can see easily in the dark of deep water. Roach do not have particularly acute eyesight. I intended feeding the bread into the swim as finely mashed up crumb, so that it fell in a white cloud onto the bottom. The question was: How much to introduce? With so few roach, it would be easy to overdo matters and over-face the fish with a glut of groundbait. There was also even the risk that a surfeit might be left to rot on the bottom and sour the whole pool. Equally, if I did not put in sufficient quantities, the roach might not be tempted away from their natural diet to the artificial one and the bread would go totally ignored. However, I was back that evening, starting the baiting regime with three slices of bread. These I wetted, pulped and fed in at the top of the pool, so that the bait would come to rest midway down it.

I continued this routine late each afternoon for two weeks. Even if the roach were not impressed by my offerings, the other wildlife certainly

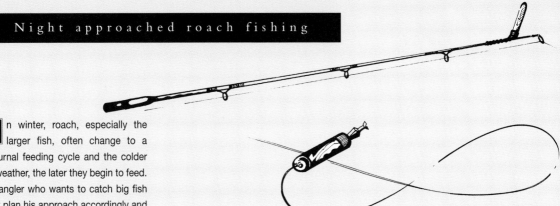

In winter, roach, especially the larger fish, often change to a nocturnal feeding cycle and the colder the weather, the later they begin to feed. The angler who wants to catch big fish must plan his approach accordingly and only go out on a river or still water as darkness falls. At night, roach may move into deeper holes, especially in waters where the current is slightly slacker.

Breadflake is the ideal bait because it is easily visible at night and roach love its smell. It is also easy to pre-bait with bread. Wet and mash a few slices and throw these into the water to settle around the hook-bait. Do not overfeed: feeding spells are often quite short and roach find a build-up of bread on the bottom very off-putting. This is a crucial point – it is far better to underfeed than to overfeed.

Tackle must be sensitive but absolutely reliable as bites are likely to be few and far between. To lose a fish is an immense disappointment. Line should have a breaking strain of three or four pounds and the hook should be size 8 or 10 to accommodate a good-sized piece of breadflake. Usually the nocturnal roach angler will be legering and, in these cases, an isotope bobbin on the quivertip indicates the bite very well. However, as long as the current is not too swift, a butt indicator produces less resistance to a taking roach and, therefore, allows the angler to time his strike perfectly. Again, an isotope bobbin can be clipped on to the line between the reel and the first ring and held down, if necessary, by added weights. For very long sessions use a bite alarm as a front rod-rest.

This can be an exciting form of fishing, especially when very large roach are being hunted. However, do keep warm: from October onwards temperatures plummet at night and it's easy to lose concentration when you are cold.

Roach are very much creatures of habit and like to live their lives according to a fixed pattern. Therefore, the more nights that you spend on a swim, feeding in bread and fishing intensively, the more results you should have. Campaigns like this might start slowly but after a month or so, all things being equal, bites should become more and more frequent. You will also find that bites become more confident as the roach consume more bread. In fact, after a while, you will have to strike at the slightest indication because often the roach will suck in the bread, chew it and swallow it without moving off at all. Why should they move? It doesn't make sense for them to bolt off every time they have sucked in what they see as a perfectly safe food item.

Finally, a tip or two about the bait itself. Always use the freshest bread possible and nip it to the shank of the hook so that the bulk of it remains fluffy. It should, however, sink quite well and stay on the hook for at least twenty minutes. I find that it pays to make a cast every twenty-five minutes or so as the roach seem to prefer it when the bread is at its softest.

LEFT: A layer of mist, unmelted by the sunlight still trying to flood into the valley, covers everything. Bait or fly can be used on such a morning but presentation has to be very precise.

ABOVE: A devastatingly cold morning after a night of snow, wind and heavy frost. A cold mist swirls across the upland valley; few fish will be feeding on a day like this. Roach will have gone off the feed, the odd chub or two may fall but only grayling will be eager for a bait.

ABOVE: A lovely roach with the stick float and maggot that led to its capture. There are times, usually when the water is low, clear and cold, when the bites are very sensitive and roach have to be worked for. This was one of those occasions.

was. I soon realized that the crumbs which I left on the bank were attracting a number of mice. They, in turn, had proved irresistible to the two barn owls working the river bank in that area. Within a week a badger living on the sandy knoll above had also discovered the new food source and I found that I was leaving a couple of slices of bread out for him too. But would the roach be so co-operative? I was without a bite or sign of a roach for thirty-three sessions from late October to the start of December, proving just how contrary the species can be. I was on the point of forsaking the ancient mill pool and trying my luck elsewhere when, one glorious evening, the buzz indicator crept towards the butt. I struck and the rod hooped over and I was into a big fish.

In the torchlight, I realized what an extraordinary creature it was. It was a very big roach, but not quite the three-pounder that I had set my heart on. What was tragically impressive, however, were the ravages of columnaris wreaked all over this erstwhile lovely fish. The disease had eaten away the dorsal fin; the scales were pock-marked and scattered and half the gill-flap had been eroded.

That first fish heralded an amazing run of roach. Between December and March I took fish on most sessions, averaging about four a week. They were all different fish and all reassuringly large. Then, just before the season's end, my first and longed for three-pound fish finally floundered into my net. It brought the episode to a close and fulfilment to a dream. I had never come to understand a fish species as deeply as I had done during that winter campaign and the lessons that I learned have proved to be pointers to roach behaviour ever since.

Almost invariably those roach fed only after dark. The only exception was when the river was turbid, with visibility less than 20 centimetres and the air temperature was 10°C and rising – an unusual combination for an English winter. Generally, the colder the weather, the later the roach began to feed. If the night was mild you could expect a fish to take the bait around an hour or so after darkness had fallen. If there was a hard frost, however, it was often necessary to wait four or even five hours: sometimes even until a perishing midnight. What you could almost guarantee, however, was that at sometime a fish would succumb.

There were certainly fish in the swim throughout the hours of waiting for a bite. There would be constant tremors on the line as they milled around, their bodies brushing the terminal tackle, but this did not necessarily mean that a bite was imminent. In fact, the fish only had a very short feeding spell and it was rare to catch more than one fish in the session, although perhaps the fight of the fish in such a confined area scared away the other members of the shoal for the rest of that night.

There were frequent surprises. One particular night, there was a freezing east wind and temperatures dropped like a stone. A fish came to the surface and began to take pieces of floating bread from an eddy at my feet. There was no doubt that it was a roach and its behaviour was plain to see and although I immediately tried introducing a slowly sinking piece of bread on the hook, this was ignored. On another occasion, on a particularly mild day, there was a hatch of sedges and at least three different large fish rolled on the surface taking the insects as they emerged. This is behaviour I have seen neither before nor since and it serves as a reminder that no one can ever know completely how fish are going to behave. Different species have their own behavioural tendencies, but fish are never more than generally predictable and individuals will frequently surprise you.

December 23rd 1995. The River Dove beneath the Izaak Walton Hotel, in the shadow of Thorp Cloud. After a freezing night, the day dawns cold, with drifting fog veiling weak sunlight. Throughout the day, air temperatures hover around freezing.

Could this possibly be the same grayling that had thwarted me on a similar frozen day in December 1994? I knew in my heart that it was: it was in the same lie beneath the bridge where the river narrows and deepens. It was the same size: around a pound-and-a-half and ounces heavier than any of the others in the shoal. Above all, it was the colour of this grayling that was so recognizable. Of all the grayling I have seen, in fifty rivers in a dozen countries, she was the only one ever coloured pure ivory.

She glowed in the water, her fin furling over her back, so strikingly beautiful. Once again I yearned to hold her; to see her beauty at close quarters for a moment in the wan sunlight. It was a vain hope: I knew it now, as I had that previous Christmas. There are fish in certain situations that cannot be caught by any legal angling method. Only a net or a stick

RIGHT: A fascinating shot and a test for all anglers. See if you can make out this beautiful grayling lying about 30 cm down in the water. With a little patience, you should be able to make out its eye and its huge dorsal fin. Spotting a well-camouflaged fish like this can sometimes lead to a successful catch.

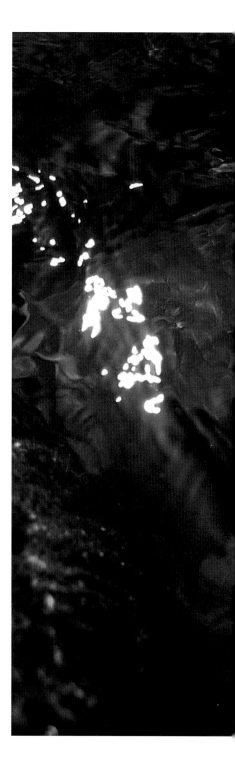

ABOVE: A lovely grayling from the River Dove lies on a thick bed of December frost.

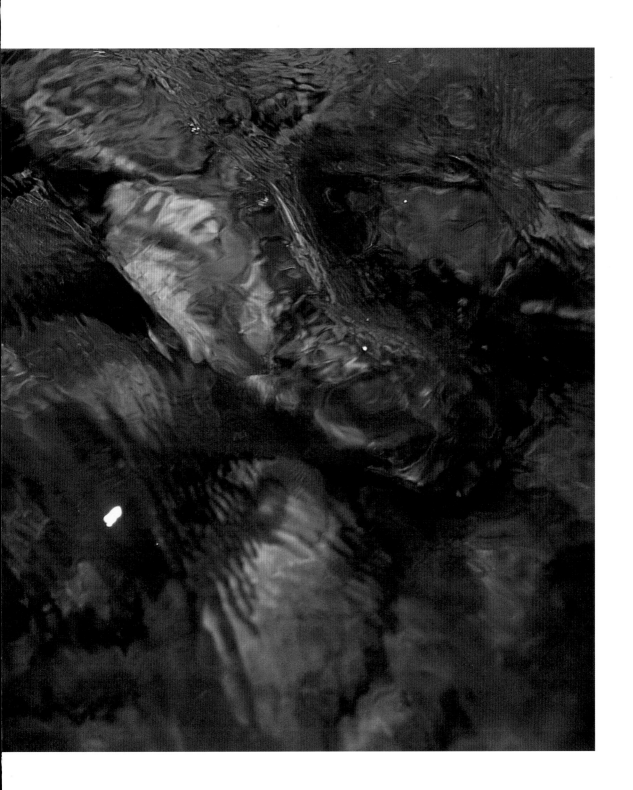

Long trotting is the perfect way to fish for grayling, which often lie as much as a hundred metres beneath the angler. There are several obvious advantages to this method of fishing. Firstly, it is an ideal way to find fish in a featureless river. If there is no response after the first dozen or so casts then it is quite in order to move on seventy or eighty metres and fish the next stretch of river if space permits. The second advantage of long trotting is that you can contact fish that are very shy and do not like close human activity, especially in fast, clear, shallow water where grayling are prevalent.

Long trotting for grayling is a fascinating way of fishing as the line must be mended continually to keep in constant control of the float. This is important because the float has to be guided towards promising areas, inched around snags and held up occasionally so that the bait rises enticingly, and then allowed to move on again with the flow of the current.

When a grayling does take, strike powerfully but gently. Keep the rod low to avoid splashing it on the surface as this will alarm the rest of the shoal and make a hook slip much more likely.

Ideal conditions for long trotting for grayling are dull overcast days with little wind. Bright sunlight produces surface glare which makes seeing the float at distance a headache-inducing job. A wind of any strengh, particularly across a stream, makes float control at long ranges very difficult.

Loose feeding can be a problem at long range. Your best bet is to feed in dribbles of mashed bread, which should perhaps be flavoured and contain maggots, casters or even pieces of chopped worm (which grayling adore). This concoction gradually dribbles down the river, persuading the grayling to feed and sometimes pulling them closer to the angler to make fishing easier. Some food may begin to float, bringing the grayling to the surface where you will see them swirl. This is an immensely exciting sight and an obvious indication of the graylings' exact location.

If fish have been spotted eighty or ninety metres away and you do not think you will spook them, then by all means move closer to them. Often long trotting is used simply as a way of finding fish and, once located, you can move in on them and fish in a more tight and delicate way. Certainly, I never really like playing a two-pound-plus grayling at long range on light tackle with a size 16 or 18 hook as the only thing linking us. During fight after fight my heart has been in my mouth absolutely every second of the fish's course to the net.

of dynamite could have brought that fish to my hand. As ever, the Dove ran as clear as air and it was hard to see how any artificial fly could succeed in deceiving fish in those conditions, no matter how skilfully it was presented.

The fish was aware of me from the moment that I walked along the frosted bank towards her, where I paused and stooped in amongst the dead rushes preparing to make a cast. When my line landed as lightly as I could make it fall and the weighted nymph dropped towards her, she arched away with such delicate determination that I knew I should never succeed. Nor would I, at least until some rain tinged the water and obscured the deficiencies in my approach, tackle and flies. Right now, that fabulous fish was about as attainable as the moon, though something like the same heavenly colour.

I made around a dozen casts to the fish, but once she was aware of my presence they didn't seem to worry her. Each time, she simply let the nymph drift past her without giving any sign of alarm or interest. How did she know I was there? Is it just the eyesight of a fish like this that is so keen; the acuteness of hearing, or the ability to pick up vibrations upon the bank? Or is there something more? In a pure, gently flowing river like the Dove this fish was obviously instantly aware the moment any angler made an attempt to catch her, especially when his fly is attached to line that must stand out like a rope to the fish. Those who do not fish, or who do not angle for visible fish, might not realize just how quickly a fish becomes aware of outside danger.

A fellow angler came towards me downriver through the mist. He was the first person I had seen since my dawn start from the sleeping hotel. He stopped by me on the bridge and we watched the fish while the sun slowly filled the valley with a misty golden light. A hundred times, he told me, he had tried to catch her and, yes, she was the same fish I had failed to catch the previous December. In fact, she had occupied the same run of water for several years now. Not once, despite every trick in the fly fisher's book, had she looked at any pattern with other than complete indifference. Perhaps a maggot might just deceive her, had the river's rules permitted it, but he was of the opinion that an artificial fly would never get the better of her.

He was happy about this. How could our grayling possibly look more beautiful out of the water than she did in it? Should anglers want to

LEFT: *A fly-caught grayling with beautiful colouring slides over the stones to the net.*

BELOW: *The Derwent at Chatsworth is one of the most lovely sights a grayling fisherman will ever see. This is a particularly productive area of water. Here the river deepens and slows and the grayling flock to it when the temperature falls. The area upstream of the bridge is particularly good, possibly because it is sheltered from the wind by the trees and high banks.*

possess, even momentarily, everything that swims? Isn't it good that there are uncatchable fish to remind us of our limitations? As we walked down the valley together, he remarked on how magically beautiful everything was that crisp morning and noted that ours were the only footsteps in the frost. To have caught and removed that particular grayling would somehow have diminished the river – and us – on this magical winter's morning. We shook hands and I turned off up the path to the hotel and breakfast and my new acquaintance disappeared away into the mist.

The River Irton, a tributary of the Wye in the heart of Wales. It is mid-March and the weather is cold and grey after heavy rain. In the river, the spate is clearing and the level falling.

Dave, Mark and Jerry could not believe their luck the Friday evening they began to fish the river. At every cast across the pool, their gold-headed nymphs were taken within seconds and another grayling would splash across the water into the net. By nightfall, each had taken at least thirty fish averaging between one and two pounds and they withdrew to the hotel feeling quite exhausted.

Next morning, the river had fined down considerably and the sun even made brief appearances, lighting up the large deep pool and revealing an extraordinary sight. The water simply teemed with grayling: far too many to count, but possibly upwards of two hundred fish were crammed into an area no larger than a tennis court. Caring anglers that they are, the trio decided to stop fishing at once, for they realized that this accumulation of fish must have been for a purpose. For now, they were content just to watch the ranks of fish lying in the current, their colours increasingly exotic in the growing light. There was a good deal to see.

One of the first things they noticed was the astounding speed at which the grayling launched themselves from the bottom of the river to take an insect from the surface. The fish rocketed vertically upwards, breaking the surface violently and, each time, leaving tell-tale bubbles. Even tiny flies were spotted by fish two metres down and, once they decided to rise, the grayling never seemed to miss. For the most part, however, the grayling stayed down on the river bottom to feed. It seemed that they were eating mostly small invertebrates, but any minnows coming close to the pool were also hunted down and taken by the larger, more active male fish.

The hotel's gardener appeared on the scene: a man with a lifetime's experience of the Wye and its tributaries. He was in no doubt that the grayling had gathered in the pool to prepare for spawning on the shallows directly above. A couple of weeks later, when the water temperatures climbed to 6°C, he was proved right. Overnight, the grayling left the deeper water and the males began to dig very shallow redds here and there for a hundred metres upstream. By this time, the males themselves had turned very dark, almost black in colour. The spot on their dorsal fins had also become more striking and distinct, possibly to be used as a signal to warn off other males intent on mating with the same female.

The spawning period of the grayling was short and hectic and the legion of fish was divided into smaller groups, with several males vying for each female. Once a male reached position next to his mate, he would curl his great dorsal fin over the hen fish, to help him maintain position in the current as he fertilized her flowing eggs with his milt.

The females each laid between three and five thousand eggs: a food source that turned the shallows into pandemonium for the days to come. Brown trout and chub burrowed into the redds, scenting out the eggs and chivvying the grayling as they spawned. At night the eels appeared, 'hoovering' up all the eggs they could find, as well as any bullhead or loach that had also been attracted by the spawning. Herons were there too as darkness fell, knowing that food would be easily come by.

The eggs that survived all these different onslaughts hatched two to three weeks later and the tiny alevins immediately hid in the gravels, away from the chub that were still combing the area for what leftovers they could find. With mating over, the adult grayling broke up into small shoals and returned to their normal haunts up and down the river. When the three anglers arrived back on the river in June, they found the fish as infuriatingly difficult to catch as ever.

Chapter 9

Ferox Trout
To Be a Fisherman

FEROX. WHAT A NAME FOR A FISH! IT ALMOST SENDS A shiver down the spine. And the fish lives up to its name: a ferocious, predatory brown trout, with leopard markings. It makes its home in the wildest glacial lakes of Britain, where it has survived for ten thousand years. As a quarry, the ferox presents the angler with the most daunting challenge.

The ferox is a unique strain of brown trout, breeding separately from normal brown trout. A typical Highland brown trout lives for around six years, while ferox can easily treble that span. A brown trout grows for about three years and then slowly declines. Ferox, on the other hand, can grow for twelve or more years: piling on weight at the age normal browns are dying. A good Highland brown trout weighs eight to twelve ounces. Ferox will commonly weigh several pounds. Eight pounds may be considered average; fifteen pounds is getting large, while thirty pounds or more is possible. The Victorian record was 39½ pounds and there are fish of that size alive today.

Along with genetic predisposition, the difference in size between ordinary brown trout and ferox is principally to do with food and food conversion. Brown trout feed primarily on insects and other invertebrates, whilst adult ferox feast almost exclusively on fish.

In Scotland, at least, the lives of the ferox trout and Arctic char (*Salvelinus alpinus*) are inextricably linked. Elsewhere, other prey species such as smelt and the various whitefish may be of more importance, but in Scotland Arctic char are the ferox's staple food. It is feared that stocks of char could be under threat in certain areas and with them, the ferox. Glacial lakes that have existed for over ten thousand years are being altered as forestry, agricultural and urban developments reshape the face of Scotland. These deep, cold waters are undergoing their first real traumas for millennia. Even if they are not under any immediate threat,

LEFT: This portrait of a ferox loch in March, the start of the season, shows a frightening prospect. Large predatorial trout will be found at depth. It is not until May, when the water temperature has risen to 10°C or 12°C, that the ferox move nearer the surface and begin to hunt more actively.

ferox must still be regarded as rare creatures, occupying the top niche of very localized food webs. Today, probably no more than a couple of hundred waters in the British Isles host the ferox and as some of these may have populations numbered in dozens only, as it is as well to realize just how precious these fish are.

It was the Victorian sportsmen who really discovered ferox trout: those pioneering souls who began to travel north from the 1830s onwards. These were hard men, used to living off the land, and sleeping rough. They visited areas where Englishmen were treated with contempt or even outright hostility, for the Stuart Rebellions had taken place only a few generations earlier. Despite their relatively primitive tackle, these early fishermen had great success. The ferox was more common then than now and the waters almost untouched by man's other encroachments. Ferox fishing is undoubtedly harder now. Changes in the environment and generations of anglers have seen to that.

To catch ferox today, anglers have to have more knowledge than their Victorian forebears, if not quite the same stamina and fortitude. Travelling is easier nowadays and accommodation more comfortable, while outboard engines have largely replaced oars. Nevertheless, a loch can still be a dreadful place to fish when the wind rises and an April sleet lashes down. Nine trips out of ten on a ferox loch may be hard and uncompromising, but there is often beauty also. Even at the end of the harshest day, the last of the sun may slip beneath the clouds and set the water on fire. And there are always those magic days when, somewhere down deep, a fish eventually takes your lure and you are finally attached to one of the miracles of the aquatic world.

July. The White Loch in Scotland's Wester Ross is seven miles long, a mile wide and up to a hundred metres deep. The day is one of rain and squally winds with very occasional bursts of sunshine. Daytime air temperatures are about 10°C, with water temperatures of around 14°C, but slowly falling.

It is 4.30 a.m. – it is important to be out early on the loch. The Victorians believed that ferox fed mostly at night; digested their kill through the day and only started looking for food again towards evening. They were wrong! Dawn is a prime time for catching a ferox, but in a remote area like this it is desperately hard to get out early unless you spend the night in the boat, or sleep rough on the hill or in a bothy. Such nights can hold terrors both imagined and real. If there is little breeze, on a warm muggy night after rain, the midges can drive you absolutely insane. At the first sight of the sun, the horseflies take over: droning in off the heather to suck one's blood. They never seem satisfied with less than a cupful of mine! The safest haven from these insects is in a boat, well away from shore and with a good wind to scatter them. This day, there is a westerly blowing the length of the loch.

I am never sure about how important wind is in ferox fishing. The Victorians swore that a real gale was necessary to stir up the loch and get the ferox on the move, but I have had great success when the water has been like a millpond. In fact, it looked as though it was going to be like that last night which was incredibly still until about 2.00 a.m.

Sounds travel a long way in this silent landscape. During the night there was a constant scuffling in the rocks behind me, but after the long walk in over the hill I was too tired to get up and investigate. At first light, the paw prints told the story. A badger had come down from the moor, probably sniffing out the rations I had had to bring with me.

In the fifteen years or so that I have been ferox fishing, most of my earlier preconceptions have been shattered. What is more, I have no hard and fast theories to take their place. Sitting about fifty metres offshore, I watch the water as the daylight grows, trying to imagine what the fish are up to. It is an awesome place: looking up a thousand metres to the tops of the mountains and then down onto the leaden water that one knows plunges to depths of a hundred metres or more. One can't see either end of the loch and even the far bank is lost in the gloom. There is no other boat on the loch and even this one had to be towed in for ten miles over the heather. I sit alone on a cauldron of water in this vast crater in the mountains. If ever I had wanted mystery and challenge in my fishing, then the White Loch ferox provide an ample supply of both.

It is a theory of mine that ferox are alerted to the presence of an angler the very moment that a boat engine is cranked into life. These are wary fish with the most acute hearing and the sound of the motor bounces off the sheer rock walls of the loch and travels through the crystal water, without any sort of muffling. The churning of a propeller must strike a discordant note in waters as remote as this. I try to use the engine as little as possible: just to take me up the loch, against the wind.

ABOVE: Dawn is the best time for ferox fishing, especially when the water is dead calm. At dawn the fish are very close to the surface and it is not unusual to see them strike into a shoal of dimpling char. The old belief that ferox always fed at great depths is quite untrue; these fish, like any big hunters, are opportunists and will take prey wherever they can find them.

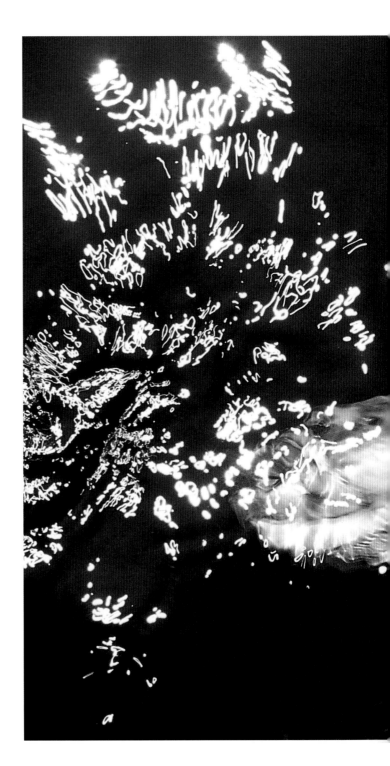

RIGHT: A ferox strikes with the most exceptional power and fury. Unlike the pike, its narrow jaws are not ideal for seizing struggling fish. However, what the ferox lacks in design, it makes up for with speed and ferocity.

Whatever the level of a person's angling skills, successful trolling will largely depend on good boat handling. If you are new to this game, go out with an experienced boatman a few times until you have learnt the ropes. Quite apart from considerations of safety, boat fishing is best done with a compatible companion anyway. Fishing can be done more efficiently with a sensible division of labour: one angler managing the fishing tackle, while the other looks after the boat.

Safety is of paramount importance. A large windswept loch can be almost as rough and as dangerous as the sea. Boat handling must be competent (at least) and safety precautions appropriate. Even in summer, a large exposed loch can be transformed from a gentle ripple to a heavy swell, with racing white horses, easily in under half an hour.

Always wear a life jacket or buoyancy aid of some sort. In spring and autumn – when it can be pretty raw in the North – a proper marine 'flotation suit' makes good sense. Such garments provide buoyancy and protection against hypothermia should you capsize or fall overboard. They also offer excellent protection in foul weather. A hundred pounds or so seems pretty cheap for something that could save your life.

Blind faith in outboard motors is misplaced. Always take oars and rowlocks! Check the fuel tank before setting out and take extra fuel if there is even the slightest chance of it being needed. Most experienced boat anglers would never venture far from the jetty without a few essential spares (split pins, shear pins, and so on) and the modicum of tools to deal with running repairs and minor emergencies.

Bodily comfort and safety afloat is usually no more than common sense. Always take sufficient warm clothing and weather protection. You can always remove a layer or two if it gets too hot, but a cold wet angler doesn't fish effectively even if he does stick it out for any length of time. In summer, hats, sunglasses and sun block cream are essential. Take plenty to drink: at least three litres of plain water on a hot summer's day. Avoid alcohol as it causes dehydration in hot weather; exacerbates exposure in cold conditions and can cloud judgement at any time.

Boat anglers should follow the sound practice of telling a responsible person (preferably backed up with a written note) where they intend going and roughly when they envisage returning.

Safety is really to do with an attitude of mind. The direst consequences can usually be avoided by good preparation; taking sensible precautions; not taking unnecessary risks and – above all – reacting calmly and without panic should something untoward occur.

Life Jacket
Check fuel tank
Check over boat and secure tackle
Fresh Water
Split and shear pins
First Aid
Hat
Sun block and sunglasses
Clothing
Estimated time of return.

Thereafter, I will cut the motor and drift down with the wind, using only the oars for navigational adjustments. A clumsy splash with an oar will probably merge unnoticed amongst the natural sounds of trout rising and waves lapping on rocks. Today it should be possible to troll two miles of the loch shore on each drift and, with two rods out, I will be covering a fair swathe of water.

Finding ferox in a water like this is a slog. The Victorians reckoned that one had to row about three hundred miles for every ferox hooked. I know that I'll have blisters before nightfall. At one time I thought that ferox would behave like typical trout in guarding a particular lie over protracted periods: a rock from behind which to ambush prey, for example. I now know better. Ferox are more like sharks, always on the move. They either actively swim about or simply drift along with the underwater currents in a never-ending search for the shoals of char. Anyone unfamiliar with large lakes will probably not appreciate the extent to which wind can create currents in them. A loch is rarely a 'still water' for there are nearly always sinews of moving water beneath the surface. Even during rare periods of calm, there is usually movement of some kind under the surface.

I like to work my lures as slowly as possible, reasoning that the ferox are more likely to attack an easy prey. When these large fish charge into a shoal of char they do so either to panic the prey fish, so that scattered and disoriented individuals can be picked off, or to cause actual physical injury. In the latter case, the ferox can return to mop up any casualties. My lures are chosen, therefore, to give out strong, erratic vibrations that emulate the distress signals emitted by an injured fish.

I particularly like the north shore of the White Loch where steep hills rise vertically from the water's edge, indicating precipitous drop-offs below the surface. Here, the water is littered with great jagged rocks, some sticking out above the surface. These rocky features will attract the char and, with them, their hunters. The southern shore, by contrast, is flatter and the bottom of the loch falls away more evenly with less exciting contours. Here, there is little to attract either prey or predator.

Today I am using two Kwikfish. These are robust lures moulded from tough plastic to help withstand the knocks and abrasion they will have to take among the rocks. At around 14 cm, they are about the size of your average char, while the colour matches that of a male char in his

ABOVE: The ferox's reputation as a big-headed, lank-bodied fish could not be further from the truth. A ferox in its prime is a beautiful fish – large and muscular from its diet of char.

ABOVE: The ferox population leaves the loch in late autumn and early winter and moves up the feeder streams or rivers, looking for fast, rock-strewn water to spawn.

ABOVE: This sleek, silvery ferox has been caught by an extremely well-prepared ferox fisherman! Notice the selection of plugs and spinners, vital tools of the trade, in the background. A large selection of these is needed as the preference of the ferox changes from day to day (even from hour to hour within a fishing session) as the light values change.

breeding 'plumage': dusky grey on top and violent red beneath. These lures have quite a pronounced 'action' and will dive to about seven metres. I would expect the char shoals to be at about this depth on a morning like this in mid-summer. The rods I shall be using are powerful and my reels have been freshly loaded with new 12-pound breaking strain lines. Everything has been checked and double checked, for waters as rough and rocky as these test tackle to the limit.

There are those who despise trolling and who would never fish for trout with anything but a fly. However, these anglers fail utterly to understand what this type of fishing is all about. The ferox is not a chalk stream brown trout. As an adult, it eats insects only very occasionally and you will only catch one in a blue moon using conventional fly-fishing techniques. Trolling is an angling art in its own right, requiring its own peculiar knowledge and skills. Controlling a boat in a gale with two or three rods working is far from easy. Should a ferox strike, one has to hold the boat, take in the other lines and land the fish. This is truly demanding if you are single-handed, in a heavy swell and drenched by numbing rain.

All trout have acute vision but with the ferox this is positively hawk-like. The fish's keen eyesight is vital, enabling it to pick out a group of char at depths of maybe fifty metres where little light penetrates. Even deep down, ferox can notice flaws in tackle or presentation. They certainly seem able to differentiate one lure from another. There have been times, on bright calm days, when I have watched ferox approach baits over and over again, looking at them from every angle, sometimes from just a few centimetres away. Even something as natural as a dead char will be inspected and is often rejected because something about it raises the fish's suspicions.

I work the baits as thoughtfully as I possibly can, trying to impart to them an action that I hope looks like those of a sick or injured bait fish. I may pay out a bit of line to allow the lure to sink a foot or so in the water. I might then pull up the rod to impart a little more life and speed, or jig the rod tip about, or alter the line of the boat. Any little nuance in the motion of the lure might be the one that triggers an attack from a following ferox. You simply have to think of those pieces of plastic, working seven metres beneath you, not as artificial lures, but as real fish. Like the fly fisherman, the troller is always experimenting: always thinking about a change of lure, of depth, of line or of speed.

Lunchtime comes and I am tired, aching, hungry and looking forward to the break. I beach the boat and stretch, shoulders cracking, then walk along the shoreline. By the mouth of the outflowing river, there are trails in the sand. Two otters were here, probably during the hours of darkness, chasing sea trout and salmon just up from the sea. Now the animals will probably be somewhere at the other end of the loch, sleeping away the daylight hours. It is good to sit awhile and watch the hills for red deer and the crags to the south where the eagles live. The ferox is a fish perfectly in keeping with this wild land of untamed beauty.

By the time I am afloat again the cloud cover is breaking up and I am pleased to see that the sporadic sunshine has become more frequent. There are those who swear by dark and gloomy weather for ferox fishing, but my best times have come on clear days, with perfect blue skies and the mountain tops free of cloud or mist. Sunlight seems to bring the ferox up from the depths, closer to the surface. It also warms the water a little and this can be important. Below 10°C, the ferox appear to stay deeper, feeding only spasmodically. At 12°C or 14°C the fish's metabolism is faster, it feels hungrier and is more actively seeking its prey. The only change I make is to reduce the size of lure by a centimetre or so. At less depth and in brighter conditions the smaller lure is noticed easily enough, but perhaps its imperfections are less blatant than those of a bigger lure and treated with less suspicion.

Now I am approaching the two islands and anticipation builds. This is an area of dramatic contour changes where the lake bed is up and down like a roller coaster. There are colossal rocks strewn down the side and along the bottom of the loch. The passing shoals of char are funnelled through the narrows between the islands and the loch shore and here the ferox can lie in wait and launch ambushes on their prey.

After quarter of a mile, the left-hand rod whacks round, bouncing down the boat's gunwale. I ship the oars at once and lunge for the rod handle, but my strike meets with nothing. It had to be a fish because the take was far too violent to have been the lure snagging on a rock or weed. In any case, my plug was working no more than eight metres down in water over twenty metres deep. With my heart thumping, it takes a couple of minutes before my hands stop shaking. Provided the fish wasn't jagged and frightened there is a good chance it could come again. At least I have found a hunting ferox and I know that I must cover the

LEFT: Ferox are so rarely caught that it takes a great deal of nerve to photograph one coming towards the boat! Generally, as the fish first breaks the surface, panic ensues on deck, especially if the day is wild and wet like this one.

ABOVE: This photograph screams ferox country – the wild moorland, the tweed-clad fisherman and the large, stunningly marked trout itself. This fish was caught early on a summer's morning when rain and wind were sweeping the loch. It fell to a big plug fished around six metres deep between two islands and fought for a full fifteen minutes.

same area as quickly as possible before it moves away. There could even be more than one fish, for ferox often travel in pairs or even groups of three or four as spawning time in late autumn approaches. I risk using the engine to get back onto the same drift as quickly as possible. At almost the same spot the same rod is slammed round a second time and, this time, stays there. The line cuts the surface like a knife, while the reel shrieks in protest. Inside I am trembling with excitement. This is ferox fishing at its best!

October 4th. A frosty dawn after a day of heavy rain in the Highlands. The upper River Garry is fining down after the spate. It enters the loch in a 400-metre-long glide over large boulders. There is no wind and the day promises to be crisp. The water temperature is about 11°C, having fallen a couple of degrees from the previous day.

Mid-September sees some big changes taking place in the loch. For the ferox and the fishermen, the most important of these is that the char are starting to move into the mouths of the rivers that feed the loch. Most of the char are autumn spawners and if the ferox are to continue feeding, they must follow the char into these fast-flowing shallow rivers. Some ferox like to hang back, a little offshore, intercepting the char as they move into the river mouth and back out again. Other ferox will actively hunt in the lower reaches of the river itself and it is these fish that present a particular opportunity to be caught.

Heavy rain helps to stimulate the char into ascending the rivers and over the first days of October it had poured. The Garry river itself rose 60 cm and its swollen waters thundered out into the loch. Sensing this increased flow into the loch, the char had gathered in their hundreds and had begun to move from the deep water into the shallow bay and up into the river itself. On the night of the third, a big group of char of around a pound each began to make the journey, tracked by a small group of aggressive and hungry ferox. These fish were mostly males, probably about eight years old and around seven pounds in weight.

Hunting in the river offers both advantages and disadvantages to the ferox. On the one hand, the char are more concentrated and have less room for escape. If four or five ferox attack together, then maybe a dozen char will be injured in the charge and easily picked off afterwards. The

Rods can be between nine and eleven feet, with an action strong enough to set the hooks, but not so stiff as to pull them free on either the strike or during the fight. Small multipliers or the new 'baitrunner' fixed-spool reels are ideal for trolling. Reel lines should be 12 – 15 pound test, while swivels should be strong and reliable. Check line and tackle regularly for signs of wear and tear, especially where terminal gear is prone to chafing against rocks.

Boat rod rests are an absolute boon, especially where more than one rod is being used. There are several good designs now available, which can be variously clamped onto a gunwale, thwart or transom. To be worthwhile, a boat rod rest must be capable of holding the rod securely whilst unattended. As an extra precaution, some anglers like to tether their rods to the boat with a cord.

ECHO SOUNDERS AND DOWNRIGGERS

The modern echo sounder/fish finder can reveal a great deal of useful information to the angler, thus allowing more effective fishing. Such devices can tell the angler the depth of water being fished over and allow the fisherman to follow contours and drop-offs. Certainly it is useful to know whether fish are present, or if a particular stretch of water is barren. However, contrary to what some might believe, a fish finder will not actually put fish on the hook! They are certainly useful, but they are expensive and are not absolutely essential.

A downrigger is a device that allows lures to be fished considerably deeper than could be achieved using ordinary end tackles. A downrigger typically comprises a heavy spherical weight that can be lowered on a wire cable from a small winch. The trace is attached to the downrigger weight with a quick release device. Should a fish strike, the trace can 'break away' from the downrigger, allowing the fish to be played on tackle unencumbered by heavy sinkers. A downrigger would usually only be employed for trolling at deeper than about ten metres.

LURES

There are literally thousands of artificial lures now available and many suitable for trolling for ferox. For a start, look for plugs of around 10 – 12 cm long, with silver, red or yellow bellies and dark green or black backs. These give a fair impression of the small char, perch and trout upon which ferox prey. Select brands that are tough and well proven and have a few that will go down to eight or nine metres. This should cover most of the depth range of feeding ferox. Check hooks regularly and keep them needle sharp with a small file or diamond hone.

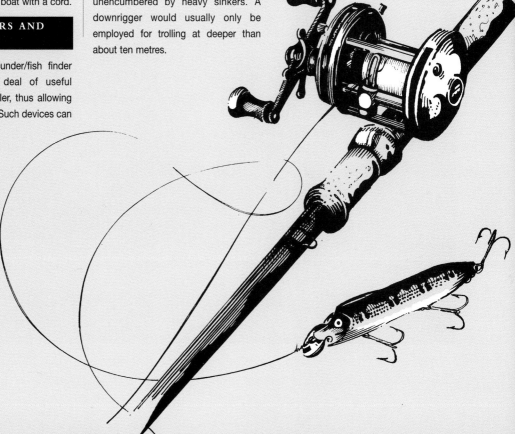

ABOVE: Christopher West holds a superb ferox fitted with
a tiny radio transmitter to monitor its movements around the
loch. It was found that this particular fish moved almost
constantly, drifting on the powerful underwater current and
looking for food. Much more is known about ferox now than
a century ago but they still remain one of freshwater fishing's
greatest enigmas.

LEFT: This is not the head of a chalk stream trout designed
to sip in mayflies. These are jaws that have dined for many
years on char of between eight ounces and one pound in weight.

down side for the ferox is that the river currents are swifter and more confused than any that they encounter in the loch. In cascading water it is easier for the big trout to mistake its timing and miss the target altogether.

I would have liked to have fished all night because, emboldened by the darkness, both char and ferox venture into the comparatively shallow water. But to do so would be dangerous work indeed. The rain-swollen river ran high and foaming and the rocks were as slippery as glass. To stumble into that spate at night would be courting death and not even ferox are worth that. Accordingly, I had set the alarm clock for a quarter-to-five. Leaving the sleeping hotel, I stride down the hillside as the very first streaks of dawn touch the eastern sky. It is a mile's treacherous walking to where the river enters the loch. My urgency is tempered with caution as I slither over wet heather and rocks and the cold lemon lights of sunrise are already spreading over Loch Garry by the time I arrive.

I am not too late. The water of a large glide erupts as a score of char scatter, skipping over the surface, with impressive bow-waves right behind them. The ferox are there and they are hungry. What makes these circumstances very special is that they are some of the few occasions that 'fly' fishing for ferox can realistically be tried. Salmon flies, reservoir lures: anything big and flashy will do. The lure I tie onto my leader is a seven-centimetre creation of hair, wool and tinsel. To human eyes it resembles nothing in particular, but I hope that it will look like a small edible fish to a ferox in the tumbling confusion of the current. For once, there are some factors on my side. Most vitally, the ferox are here to hunt and my fly is unlikely to be inspected minutely. Secondly, the river is still roaring through and the current will give realistic life to the fly, while hiding its imperfections. Moreover, a ferox will have to make a snap decision if it is to seize a passing morsel in such a swift and swirling current. The smoking autumn sun is shrouded in mist and its light is barely penetrating the surface and this too is in my favour. But I'll certainly not have everything my own way.

It is very difficult to control the fly in such a current. No sooner has it touched the water, but a belly of line is snatched by the current and the lure is pulled unnaturally across the stream. It is also very hard to get the fly deep enough in water this quick. Ideally, I should be fishing a metre beneath the surface but, more often than not, line and fly are whisked off downriver before achieving an effective depth. But should I hook a fish, then I'll really have problems! With its shovel of a tail and powerful muscular body, the ferox is a strong enough fish by any reckoning. If a large one gets up any steam and goes off downstream in a spate river like this, with no chance of following it, the game will be up. The reel will be stripped to the drum; the line will part with a crack and the ferox will be back, free, in the loch. So, whilst I might have a good chance of hooking a fish, the odds still lie most definitely with the ferox.

Back at the hotel, over breakfast, I tell the story to other anglers gathered in the dining room. The sun was already far risen and had led me to think my chance had passed. Suddenly, I had seen a ferox following my fly. The fish was huge – well over fifteen pounds – but the colouring and the shape were even more breathtaking. It had big red spots that seemed to glow on flanks of mahogany and, what impressed on me most of all, an enormous riveting eye. At first it dismissed my fly and then, seemed to turn on me with equal scorn. In that brief moment I realized, as never so clearly before, that to be a fisherman is to witness a world of never-ending wonder.

Epilogue

For a book, and a television series that have set out to explore the lives of our freshwater fish, many grey areas and some mysteries remain. Fish will always remain to some extent unknowable and their behaviour difficult to interpret. Why, for example, do river roach often have a feeding spell around midday when the water is freezing cold and the sun is shining brightly. This is the exact time when you would expect them to disappear, hide in dead sedge rather than be out hunting for food. From what we know already of roach, this makes no sense at all and yet it happens. Recently I have heard of very large fish showing up on the echo-sounders of anglers fishing Loch Lomond. These are almost certainly pike but what makes it so interesting is that they are lying at great depths – more than twenty-five metres down. What are they doing there? Are they feeding or are they just drifting with the currents, digesting their meals in the dark and cold?

We should also ask why so many fish species are growing to be larger today than in previous times. Bream and tench are perfect examples of this and the records for fish size are today almost twice what they were thirty or forty years ago. A seven-pound tench, for example, is not a rarity these days whereas in the 1950s such a weight would have been a record. A more worrying phenomenon is the burbot, a strange mottled cross between a cod and an eel, which has seemingly disappeared from our waters. The allis shad, a large migratory herring-like fish, appears to have become entirely extinct in the British Isles, even in its former strongholds the rivers Wye and Severn. Most baffling of all are the rapidly decreasing sea trout populations in the north and the west over the last decade. Is this due to food shortages or to strange illnesses, possibly associated with marine fish farms or even the nuclear power industry?

Everything that has been recorded in *Tales from the River Bank* is believed to be true today. Yet in a hundred years' time, the book could well be laughably out of date and would appear to be as full of myths and legends as Walton's 17th Century, *Compleat Angler*, seems to a modern reader. As more and more anglers and researchers are becoming fascinated with fish behaviour, knowledge is growing rapidly and dramatic discoveries are being made on a regular basis.

After watching the programmes and reading the book, it should never again be a mystery why anglers are happy to get up at dawn, to sleep on the bank all night long, or to laugh at the rain and wind, the cold and sleet, midges, bulls in the water-meadows, sunburn, stale sandwiches, constantly wet feet and all the other minor irritations that would worry someone sane. The fisherman enjoys some unique and wonderful sights, rather like the mountaineer or deep-sea diver who experience things that others can only see on a photograph or a film. Think of the smoking mere at dawn, the mist rising towards a slowly brightening sky or sunsets that turn entire lakes into shimmering cauldrons of fire. To me water is the most fascinating of all the elements: constantly changing, completely different from one day to the next, sometimes still and solemn, sometimes wind-lashed, angry, roaring, majestic and even frightening.

My aim in writing *Tales from the River Bank* has been to show fish as the beautiful and fascinating creatures that they really are. Remember the amazing coral-pink of the barbel's pectoral fins, a colour virtually impossible to recreate on an artist's palette. Think back to the marvellous mottled camouflage of a pike, the quivering black markings that bar the perch, the sheen of gold that covers the rudd and the yard of silver that is displayed when a salmon climbs a waterfall.

Throughout *Tales from the River Bank* fishing has been shown as a way to enjoy some of the most beautiful landscapes imaginable. I remember one spring evening when I was researching for filming on the River Wye. I left the river as darkness fell and the temperature dropped. I climbed the wooded bank from the water, avoiding the gnarled branches of the age-old trees, and sensed nothing unusual until I approached the crest of the hill and the path to the village. There I was struck by the most beautiful sight. Before me the foothills of the Black Mountains stretched out black as pitch, the sky above them a darkening lemon flecked with violent purple clouds. A tiny pike's tooth moon hung between the dark trees against the menacing sky. I watched, spellbound and silent, for some time and then began to walk through the wood again to the outskirts of the village. A beam of yellow light flooded the meadow path: a church service was just ending and the sound of an organ strayed along the wind. I stood at the churchyard gates listening to the footsteps of the worshippers on the gravel; it was like a scene from the past, one that an angler from hundreds of years ago would also have recognized.

Tales from the River Bank demonstrates that fishing is about passion and excitement. There are times when the angler's heart beats madly, when he can't keep his hands still and when his rod shakes uncontrollably as the line finally begins to snake out over the water. What he then feels is either pure elation as the fish is landed or an almost inconsolable sadness if it breaks free.

All great sportsmen show perfectly co-ordinated physical skills but what is amazing about fishing is the amount of technique involved. To be that fabled creature, 'the Complete Angler', you have to master a range of skills that would leave a cricketer or a footballer floundering. One day you might be casting a tiny dry fly, the size of a gnat, hoping it will interest a wise old trout lying beneath a trailing willow branch on a clear chalk stream. The next night, you could be wading a Welsh river in total darkness, your line hissing backwards and forwards just out of reach of the bats in the branches. Then, one freezing day in March, you could be on the swollen Tay trying to present a fly or spinner to a salmon that is lying on the bottom of a pool as deep as a house and as violent as an erupting volcano. In summer, you might be stalking carp; in the autumn plug fishing for perch; and then, as winter comes, you may be using any one of a dozen tactics for pike fishing in either a river or a lake.

I hope that with *Tales from the River Bank* I have finally disproved the old adage of fishing as nothing more that a worm at one end of the line and a fool at the other. Anglers all over the country deserve their rightful portrayal as sensitive and caring naturalists and, with *Tales from the River Bank*, I hope to have done them justice.

Bibliography

General

The Fishing Detective,
John Bailey, HarperCollins, 1994.

Freshwater Fishing,
F. Buller and H. Falkus, Stanley Paul, 1988.

The Great Anglers,
John Bailey, David & Charles, 1990.

Living Waters,
O. Alexandersson, Gateway Books, 1985.

The New Complete Angler,
S. Downes, Orbis, 1983.

Red Letter Days,
Ed. P. Rogers, Crowood Press, 1994.

Chapter 1 Barbel and Chub

The Complete Barbel Angler,
R. Miller, Crowood Press, 1996.

In Search of Big Chub,
T. Miles, Crowood Press, 1996.

Quest for Barbel,
T. Miles and T. West, Crowood Press, 1986.

Chapter 2 Trout

A Guide to Aquatic Trout Food,
Dave Whitlock, Swan Hill Press, 1995.

A Guide to River Trout Flies,
John Roberts, Crowood Press, 1989; paperback 1995.

In Search of Wild Trout,
Nicholas Fitton, Ward Lock, 1992.

The Trout – A Fisherman's Natural History,
Rupert Watson, Swan Hill Press, 1993.

The Trout and the Fly – A New Approach,
B. Clarke and J. Goddard, Benn, 1980.

Chapter 3 Carp

Carp – Quest for the Queen,
J. Bailey and N. Page, Crowood Press, 1986.

Casting at the Sun,
Christopher Yates, Pelham, 1986.

Redmire Pool,
L. Arbury and K. Gifford, Beekay, 1984.

Successful Carp Fishing,
J. Cundiffe, Crowood Press, 1995.

Chapter 4 Salmon

The Lives of Salmon,
Alan Youngson and David Hay, Swan Hill Press, 1996.

Salmon and Women,
W. Patterson and P.B. Behan, Witherby, 1990.

Tragedy of the Salmon,
D. Shaw, Hillfield Press, 1995.

Chapter 5 The Eel

The Eel,
C. Moriaty, David & Charles, 1978.

Chapter 6 Pike

The Art of Lure Fishing,
C. Bettell, Crowood Press, 1994.

The Domesday Book of Mammoth Pike,
F. Buller, Stanley Paul, 1979.

Pike,
F. Buller, MacDonald & Co., 1971.

Pike Fishing – The Practice and the Passion,
M. Brown, Crowood Press, 1993.

Pike – The Predator Becomes the Prey,
J. Bailey and N. Page, Crowood Press, 1985.

A Piker's Progress,
J. Watson, Creel, 1991.
How to catch Bigger Pike from Loch, Lakes and Rivers,
Paul Gustafson HarperCollins, 1997

Chapter 7 Tench, Rudd and Still-water Species

The Book of the Perch,
P. Rogers and S. Burke, The Perch Fishers' Oxford Illustrated Press, 1991.

Fish of the Summer Still Waters,
J. Bailey, Crowood Press, 1989.

In Pursuit of Big Tench,
Len Arbury, Crowood Press, 1996.

Chapter 8 Roach and Grayling

Coarse Fishing,
M. Hayes, Crowood Press, 1995.

Grayling – The Fourth Game Fish,
Ed. Dr R. Broughton, Crowood Press, 1989.

Roach the Gentle Giants,
J. Bailey, Crowood Press, 1987.

Chapter 9 Ferox

Casting for Gold,
J. Bailey, Crowood Press, 1990.

Ferox and Char,
R. P. Hardy, Oliver and Boyd, 1940.

In Wild Waters,
J. Bailey, Crowood Press, 1988.

Index